# *12 Strategies from Heaven*
## For the Ekklesia

DEBBIE BILEK

Also by Debbie Bilek:

*Smiling on the Outside, Dying on the Inside*

*Strategies from Heaven: Contending for the Impossible*

12 STRATEGIES FROM HEAVEN for the Ekklesia © 2020 by Debbie Bilek.

All rights reserved. Printed in the USA.

Published by Author Academy Elite
P.O. Box 43, Powell, OH 43065
www.AuthorAcademyElite.com

All rights reserved. This book contains material protected under International and Federal Copyright Laws and Treaties. Any unauthorized reprint or use of this material is prohibited. No part of this book may be reproduced or transmitted in any form or by any means, electronic or mechanical, including photocopying, recording, or by any information storage and retrieval system, without express written permission from the author.

Identifiers:

**Library of Congress Control Number: 2020901686**

Paperback: 978-1-64746-131-7

Hardback: 978-1-64746-132-4

Ebook: 978-1-64746-133-1

Available in paperback, hardback, e-book, and audiobook.

All Scripture quotations, unless otherwise indicated, are taken from the Holy Bible, New International Version®, NIV®. Copyright © 1973, 1978, 1984 by Biblica, Inc.™ Used by permission of Zondervan. All rights reserved worldwide.

Scripture quotations marked HCSB are taken from the Holman Christian Standard Bible®, Copyright © 1999, 2000, 2002, 2003 by Holman Bible Publishers. Used by permission. Holman Christian Standard Bible®, Holman CSB®, and HCSB® are federally registered trademarks of Holman Bible Publishers.

Scripture quotations marked TPT are taken from The Passion Translation® Copyright © 2017, 2018 by Passion & Fire Ministries, Inc. Used by permission. All rights reserved. ThePassionTranslation.com

Scripture quotations marked ESV are taken from The Holy Bible, English Standard Version. ESV® Text Edition: 2016. Copyright © 2001 by Crossway Bibles, a publishing ministry of Good News Publishers.

Scripture quotations marked NASB are taken from the New American Standard Bible, Copyright © 1960, 1962, 1963, 1968, 1971, 1972, 1973, 1975, 1977, 1995 by The Lockman Foundation. Used by permission.

Scripture quotations marked King James 2000, KJV, NKJV, AKJV, CSB, BSB, or NLT are taken from https://biblehub.com. Accessed 2018, 2019.

Any internet addresses (websites, blogs, etc.) and telephone numbers printed in this book are offered as a resource. They are not intended in any way to be or imply an endorsement by Author Academy Elite, nor does Author Academy Elite vouch for the content of these sites and numbers for the life of this book.

Book design by Jetlaunch. Cover design by Debbie O'Byrne.

# *Dedication*

This book is dedicated to the Ekklesia, those who are arising in strength and power as temples of the living God and dominion stewards of the earth. Thank you for your efforts and sacrifice in bringing heaven to earth.

A very special thank you to my brothers and sisters of the underground church across the globe. Your testimonies and real life encounters stretch me, challenge me, convict me, and leave me breathless on my knees. You are fearless frontline warriors who have laid it all down for the cause of glorifying Jesus above all else. I honor you. You are the true heroes.

# Table of Contents

Acknowledgments . . . . . . . . . . . . . . . . . . . . . . . . . . . . .ix

A Note to the Reader. . . . . . . . . . . . . . . . . . . . . . . . . . .xi

Introduction: What is the Ekklesia? . . . . . . . . . . . . . . . .xiii

Chapter 1: Prophesy . . . . . . . . . . . . . . . . . . . . . . . . . . . 1

Chapter 2: Decree the Word . . . . . . . . . . . . . . . . . . . . . 9

Chapter 3: Worship. . . . . . . . . . . . . . . . . . . . . . . . . . . 19

Chapter 4: Pray. . . . . . . . . . . . . . . . . . . . . . . . . . . . . . 27

Chapter 5: Pray in the Spirit . . . . . . . . . . . . . . . . . . . . 35

Chapter 6: Give Thanks. . . . . . . . . . . . . . . . . . . . . . . . 45

Chapter 7: Forgive . . . . . . . . . . . . . . . . . . . . . . . . . . . 55

Chapter 8: The Blood of Jesus . . . . . . . . . . . . . . . . . . 65

Chapter 9: Generational Sin and Curses. . . . . . . . . . . . . 71

Chapter 10: Anointing Oil & Prayer Cloths. . . . . . . . . . 79

Chapter 11: Fast for Breakthrough. . . . . . . . . . . . . . . . . 85

Chapter 12: Become a Radically Generous Giver . . . . . . 93

Conclusion: Your Call to Action . . . . . . . . . . . . . . . . . 101

Discussion Points . . . . . . . . . . . . . . . . . . . . . . . . . . . 105

Notes . . . . . . . . . . . . . . . . . . . . . . . . . . . . . . . . . . . . 119

About the Author . . . . . . . . . . . . . . . . . . . . . . . . . . 121

# Acknowledgments

Thank you to the Father, Son, and Holy Spirit. What a beautiful, life-long journey of getting to know you more intimately with each new day. You are my rock, my shield, my defender, my Savior, my teacher, my healer, my counselor, and my very best friend. Without you, I am nothing. With you, I can do all things.

Thank you to Patricia King, Robert Hotchkin, Stacey Campbell, Graeme and Sabrina Walsh, the Santa Maria Valley Healing Rooms and Apostolic Training Center, and Kary Oberbrunner with his Igniting Souls Tribe. You are the experts at:

- Equipping
- Training
- Sending
- Building

- Empowering
- Mentoring
- Teaching
- Loving sacrificially
- Lighting a fire under me.

The words "thank you" do not adequately express the deep gratitude I have for each of you and the many ways you have encouraged me to fulfill my God-given destiny.

A huge thank you to my editor, Kristi Ryan, for the countless hours spent using your detailed eye and expertise to bring this project to completion. You are gifted. Keep using your giftings for Jesus all the days of your life!

And lastly, I acknowledge my faithful life partner, the one who works hard each day to support me in every way so that I am freed up to do what the Lord has called me to do… My beloved husband, Bill. My life is all the richer with you at my side. Thank you for making me a better person every day. I will love you forever.

# A Note to the Reader

This is a special version of my original book *Strategies from Heaven* that is specifically designed for the Ekklesia. I've incorporated the same timeless, biblical strategies and stories in a shorter version for ease of reference, with some modifications. Each chapter is titled with the corresponding strategy for quick access when needing to immediately implement a specific battle plan.

I encourage you to go through this book with a group of believers for accountability and to walk out your corporate destiny. There is incredible value in going through life with those who are not afraid to sharpen you, pull you higher, partner with you, and challenge you to grow. Please refer to the *Discussion Points* at the back of this book which are included for this very purpose.

Reference these strategies over and over when you are under attack. They will push back darkness, keep you grounded in the mind of Christ, and pull you to victory time and time again.

I'm cheering you on as you occupy enemy territory to bring heaven to earth. True transformation will come to you, your family, your circle of influence, your region, and ultimately the world, as you walk out these heavenly strategies.

To God be the glory!!!

INTRODUCTION

# What is the Ekklesia?

*You were not created to just survive and affect a few lives around you. You are here to transform communities, regions, and nations!*

YOU are the Ekklesia! What does that even mean? The Greek noun *Ekklesia* is a compound of the preposition *ek*, which means "out of," and the verb *kaleo*, meaning "to call." Thus, Ekklesia literally means "called out ones." If you are a believer in Jesus Christ, you are one who has been called out. Did you hear that? You are chosen! You have been selected to walk the earth for this season to fulfill a divine purpose.

The Ekklesia (Greek: ἐκκλησία) was the principal assembly of the democracy of ancient Athens. The assembly was responsible for declaring war, implementing military strategy, and electing other officials. Ekklesia has been commonly translated "The Church," but that translation gives the reader a watered-down version of the power and responsibility of the true Ekklesia.

It is time for the Ekklesia to arise unto its true standing in the world. Isaiah 9:6 reports, "For to us a child is born, to us a son is given, **and the government will be on His shoulders.** And He will be called Wonderful Counselor, Mighty God, Everlasting Father, Prince of Peace" (emphasis mine). Jesus came to rule and to reign. As a child of God, you are called to rule and to reign with Him (Revelation 5:10), to usher in the Kingdom of God. "The Kingdom of God is… righteousness, peace and joy in the Holy Spirit" (Romans 14:17).

How do we usher in the Kingdom of God? It comes from within as we pursue deep intimacy with the Holy Spirit. I urge you to yield to the call. We have entered an exciting new season. Every believer has the opportunity to engage in the fullness of all that is to come. There are no bystanders in this next age. It will take every believer, activated and mobilized in their unique gifting, to meet the demand of the harvest that is upon us.

It is time for the Ekklesia, the governing Body of Christ, to rise up and stand out. If we continue to look like the rest of the world, why would anyone be drawn to us or to Jesus in us? We are called to change society, not allow society to change us. We must enter into that place of relentless intimacy with the Holy Spirit as our counselor, teacher, comforter, guide, and best friend. His voice should be louder than any other voice in our heads. We must yield to conviction and raise our standard to the place of sold-out obedience. True righteousness can only come through the precious blood of Jesus Christ. The Lord is calling us to a standard of holiness that He made possible when He died for our sins, returned to the Father, and left us His Holy Spirit.

> *We are called to change society, not allow society to change us.*

I am extending a challenge to the church to rise up and walk in the authority and anointing given freely to us when the Father sacrificed His only beloved Son for the sake of the world. It is time to be bold in our faith, take the Kingdom by force, and become the pure, spotless Bride of Christ. The time is now to make ourselves ready for His return. We must spend quality time in the secret place with God, listening to His heart. This will equip us to invest, reach out, disciple, and prepare all who will heed the call. It's time to live out Matthew 10:8:

> Heal the sick, raise the dead, cure those with leprosy, and cast out demons. Give as freely as you have received! (NLT)

Will you set aside your earthly agenda? Are you ready to die to yourself and live for Christ? I remind you it will not be easy, but it will be worth every moment of temporary suffering when you begin walking in the fullness of knowing our Lord and sharing daily intimate encounters with Him. A day is coming when:

> At the name of Jesus every knee should bow, in heaven and on earth and under the earth, and every tongue acknowledge that Jesus Christ is Lord, to the glory of God the Father. (Philippians 2:10-11)

I summon you to begin activating the biblical strategies in this book to bring the Kingdom of Heaven to earth. This is your moment in time where destiny meets purpose and you become more alive than you ever dreamed possible. It's time to arise and shine for the glory of the Lord is upon you!

> Rise up in splendor and be radiant, for your light has dawned and Yahweh's glory now streams from you! Look carefully! Darkness blankets the earth, and thick gloom covers the nations, but Yahweh arises upon you and

the brightness of His glory appears over you! Nations will be attracted to your radiant light and kings to the sunrise-glory of your new day. Lift up your eyes higher! Look all around you *and believe,* for your sons are returning from far away and your daughters are being tenderly carried home. Watch as they all gather together, eager to come back to you!

Then you will understand and be radiant. Your heart will be thrilled and swell with joy. The fullness of the sea will flow to you and the wealth of the nations will be transferred to you! (Isaiah 60:1–5 TPT)

# CHAPTER 1

## *Prophesy*

> *Pursue love and desire spiritual gifts, and above all that you may prophesy.*
>
> 1 Corinthians 14:1 (HCSB)

Last year I experienced a miracle that I never want to forget. It revealed to me the heart of the Father, how intimately He knows and pursues each of His children. It was a Thursday afternoon and I had been engaged in ministry an hour from home. As I left the meeting, I texted my husband letting him know I was getting on the road. He responded by suggesting that I stop by to have lunch with him at his work site. We met at a local restaurant. The hostess greeted us as we walked in and seated us in a room to the right of the entrance where three gentlemen were softly conversing at a nearby table.

As we were deciding what to order, I felt a tugging in my spirit like I was supposed to go over and bless one of the three men. I said to my husband, "Honey, I think I'm supposed to go over and talk to that man with his back towards us." He responded, "Okay! I'll meet you in the car!" After a good chuckle he said, "How about we eat our lunch and when we finish, if you're still feeling it, I'll go over there with you."

We finished eating and I was still feeling it, so we got up and walked over to their table. I was nervous, not really knowing what I was going to say. I only knew I was supposed to bless one of the men and tell him that the Lord loved him. When we got to their table I said, "Hi, my name is Debbie, and this is my husband Bill." Then I looked straight into the man's eyes and said, "I felt the Lord telling me to come over here to let you how much He loves you and that He is passionately pursuing you."

The other two gentlemen almost fell over! The look on their faces was one of pure astonishment! Bill and I gave each other a nervous glance. One of the men spoke up, pointing to the man I had addressed and said, "This guy was recently released from prison. I am his friend and [motioning to the other gentleman] this is his probation officer. We were just sharing the Gospel with him, telling him how much God loves him and that Jesus died for his sins. Not more than a few minutes ago, I said, 'If what we are telling you is true, God is going to send someone to confirm what we are saying to you.'" It was *minutes* later that Bill and I showed up at their table and told him how much God loved him. They were blown out of the water, while we stood there in awe of our Lord. We asked if we could pray for them and, with permission, my husband prayed over them. They then asked if they could pray for us. The waitress came over to tell us how blessed she was as the ripple effect was going out through the whole

> *The LORD directs the steps of the godly. He delights in every detail of their lives.*

restaurant. It was a joyous, amazing moment in time. The beauty is that God truly was passionately pursuing this young man who had just been set free. In that moment he knew, without a doubt, that his Father in heaven loved him personally.

I was overcome by the love of God through that encounter. I had been meditating on Psalm 37:23 that week which says, "The LORD directs the steps of the godly. He delights in every detail of their lives" (NLT). I got in the car and began praising God for His faithfulness and for how much He demonstrated His love for that lost soul. I was overwhelmed by how the Lord had orchestrated the whole thing—each and every detail. My husband and I didn't wake up that morning planning to have lunch together. I happened to get out of my meeting and texted him. He happened to be finishing up his project and encouraged me to stop by to eat with him. We met at a particular restaurant. The hostess chose to lead us to the room on the right and seated us in a specific booth near those three gentlemen. The Lord prompted my spirit to address the one man. My husband suggested we wait until after we had eaten. Had we gone when I originally wanted to, the friend would not yet have stated that God was going to send someone to confirm what they were telling him about Jesus. It was miraculous how God had ordered each of our steps to bless this child of His that had been given a fresh start in life.

## *Imagine the Impact!*

I want to encourage you when you feel that gnawing in your stomach or when God highlights somebody to you, go up to the person even if you don't know what to say. God is faithful. If you open your mouth and take a step, He is going to fill it with a blessing, a word of comfort, a word of encouragement, or an exhortation, because that's who He is and that's what He does. That is the heart of the Father. He longs to use each of you to bring hope, joy, and love to this world.

The Word of God says that we should earnestly desire all the gifts of the Spirit, but especially that we may prophesy (1 Corinthians 14:1). Prophecy is for everyone. For some, the very word "prophecy" conjures up feelings of fear or insecurity, but it is really quite simple. 1 Corinthians 14:3 teaches, "But the one who prophesies speaks to people for their strengthening, encouraging and comfort." Every one of you is wired to speak a word of encouragement, a word that will build someone up, or a word that will comfort a broken heart. Do you know how I know you have this gift? Because as a believer you have the Holy Spirit living within you. He is the great encourager and Almighty comforter.

**Can you imagine the impact on the world if every single believer went around speaking words of exhortation, encouragement, and comfort? Imagine the Bride of Christ walking into banks, grocery stores, gas stations, doctor's offices, churches, schools, government buildings, parks, restaurants, etc. and speaking the heart of the Father over everyone God sends us to! Think of the strong effect that would be taking place in your specific region if every lover of God began opening their mouths to speak love, kindness, and truth into the hearts of those walking around them. The world would be impacted in such a way as to usher the Kingdom of Heaven to earth!**

This is exactly what happened in my own life a few years ago! Strangers began approaching me everywhere I went, speaking the Word of God over me, and showing me my Father's heart—how *He* saw me. That was the beginning of my journey toward healing from the inside out. I had been sick for numerous years with fibromyalgia, chronic fatigue syndrome, Hashimoto's thyroid disease, migraine headaches, and reflex sympathetic dystrophy. As believers began prophesying over me, my body began responding and I began to heal. Words of comfort, exhortation, and encouragement began coming at me from every direction. God was pursuing me through His beautiful body, the Ekklesia. Christian men and women were coming out of the woodwork to remind me of who I was in Christ, the call on my life, and how much God loved me.

As the Father's heart reached out to me from many different avenues, my soul wounds began to heal. These were the deep internal scars that had attached themselves to me through a life of pain. As my soul began to heal, my symptoms of illness began to fall to the ground one after the other. In one short year, I progressed from being on ten prescription medications to zero! Today I am healthy, alive, vibrant, full of joy and peace. I am living the plans and purposes God has for me.

*Be the change agent in someone's healing journey!*

My life has been transformed because of prophecy—words of encouragement, exhortation, and comfort that men and women of God were bold enough to speak over me. These were ordinary people who heeded the voice of God and stepped out to share His heart. As I began to write out the words, pray over them, and read them over and over, I began to become the person that God created me to be. It has been a beautiful love story of my Father in heaven, using His body, the Ekklesia, to speak identity and destiny into my soul.

I hardly recognize myself. In just a few short years I have been delivered from a spirit of suicide, numerous illnesses, a negative mindset, and a life of barely surviving, to life abundant. My own personal deliverance has been a journey over time, but I have seen others who have been instantly set free. God is a God of grace. He meets each of us exactly where we are and knows just what we need at any given moment. You can read more of my testimony in my book, *Smiling on the Outside, Dying on the Inside*.

## *Seize the Moment*

Be the change agent in someone's healing journey! Be that voice of truth. When you feel the prompting of the Holy Spirit, ask for the grace and the boldness to address the person you are being led to speak to. Open your mouth and watch God fill it! 1 Thessalonians 5:24 says, "The One who calls you is faithful, and He will do it." I have seen Him come through time and time again. It just takes a small step of faith on our part. The worst that could happen is that the person might reject you or scoff at you, and you might feel a little foolish. The best thing that could happen is a life changed forever. The risk is worth it!

I'll never forget the day I walked into the post office to get my mail. As I passed by a woman, I felt the prompting of the Holy Spirit to address her. I began arguing with God in my head. *I'm tired. God, you know what a hard, long day I've had. I just want to go home and unwind.* I picked up my mail and proceeded to walk past her again, the same feeling welling up inside of me. What did I do? I pushed the urging aside and walked right out of the post office and got into my car. As I sat down in my nice, warm vehicle, at last ready to head home and put my feet up, I heard the still small voice of the Holy Spirit say, "Are you really going to rob my daughter of a blessing?" Ugh! Talk about conviction! I got out of the car and headed back inside, looking for the woman I had ignored, but half praying she would be gone (Ha! Ha! I was definitely battling my flesh).

I saw her standing in the same spot where I had blatantly walked past her twice. I whispered under my breath, "Okay God, I'm going to open my mouth, but You had better fill it!" How thankful I am that God did not allow me to go home without acting on His prompting. I would have missed the incredible miracle that He wanted to accomplish. A personal God reaching out to show how much He loved and cared for every intimate detail of this woman's life.

I walked up to the stranger without an ounce of faith, not a word in my heart. I only knew in my gut that the Lord had something to say. I opened my mouth and out came: "Hi, my name is Debbie. I walked past you twice, but God stopped me and wanted me to come back to find you. He wants you to know how much He loves you and that He has peace for you in the midst of the trying circumstance you are facing."

She began to weep. A brief conversation revealed that she had just come from an appointment where they had found a tumor on her breast and she was facing surgery. I asked if I could pray for her. She appeared self-conscious, her body language saying, *Right here? In the middle of the post office?* I nodded. She nodded in return, and I began to pray. This woman did not know there was a God who loved her intimately. She had never been introduced to her personal Savior who would be by her side to walk her through the road ahead. She had never met the God who could heal her.

Imagine if I had walked out and continued to drive away! I'm sure God would have used somebody else, but I would have missed the incredible joy of getting to be the hands and feet of Jesus. I would have missed the huge blessing of introducing somebody to the Lord. I got back in my car and broke down thanking God for His intense conviction. I asked Him to never let me miss it again.

Pray with me:

Lord, let us be a people who covet the gift of prophecy. Let us be Your voice to our family, friends, neighbors, co-workers, and everyone we meet. Give us divine appointments to speak Your heart to the downtrodden, to those needing a word of encouragement, to the broken-hearted, and to the influencers in our schools, the political arena, the media, and the government. Fill us each day with more and more of Your Holy

Spirit so we can become vessels of Your overflowing love, joy, peace, and righteousness. Let us reflect You in everything we say and do. Let others say of us that there is something different, something bright, something joyful, something so full of peace that there are not words to describe us. Let us stand out from the world. Set us apart to be Your holy vessels of love. Use us God, as Your hands, feet, and voice to the nations. Let us be ones who prophesy Your heart over leaders, rulers, and those in positions of influence. May we be atmosphere-shifters and destiny-changers. In Jesus' name we pray. Amen.

I decree 1 Samuel 10:6-7 over you:

> The Spirit of the LORD will control you,
> you will prophesy with them,
> and you will be transformed into a different person.
> When these signs have happened to you,
> do whatever your circumstances require,
> because God is with you. (HCSB)

## CHAPTER 2

# Decree the Word

*You will also decree a thing, and it will be established for you;
And light will shine on your ways.*

*Job 22:28, NASB*

There she sat, behind the cold, white, sterile walls of a hospital room. She had been sentenced to isolation for a month now due to a highly contagious disease. She was lonely, depressed, gravely ill, and losing hope. Thoughts of never escaping this life of isolation raced through her head almost every moment of the day. How much longer could she endure the hopelessness and despair that haunted her twenty-four seven? Had it not been for the large window in her room that looked out over the beautiful hospital gardens, giving her a connection to the outside world, I think she might have not survived what turned into a very long six-month stay.

Merri had been sick for most of her life. She struggled with numerous rare diseases which led to the amputation of one of her legs as a young adult. Wheelchair-bound and handicapped in many ways, she struggled through life as best as she could. We watched her deteriorate from an intelligent college instructor in her late twenties to a mentally unstable, physically deteriorating woman in her fifties. It had been a hard road. Few doctors had the knowledge as to how to treat her or what to do for her.

As my husband and I suited up with hospital gowns and gloves in order to be allowed to visit with her, many thoughts roamed through my head. I met Merri when I was a teenager in college. She was the sister of my boyfriend, who eventually became my beloved husband. Merri and I hit it off from the start. She had a sweet, tender spirit and was precious to me. Walking with her through the many years of deterioration was extremely painful. What could we say that would possibly cheer her up? What hope could we provide?

I sat on the bed next to her while tears streamed down her cheeks. I begged God to give me something that would cheer her up, anything that would give her hope to hold on to. I began to remind Merri of the Apostle Paul who was beaten, chained, imprisoned, and treated most unfairly. I recounted to her how this man, who was not handed a fair ride in life, went on to write much of the New Testament while behind prison walls. His words have brought healing, life, salvation, and hope to more people than we will ever be able to count through the years. I began to see a spark of encouragement in her eyes.

The Lord brought to mind a Bible verse I had recently memorized, Job 22:28, which boasts, "You will also decree a thing and it will be established for you; And light will shine on your ways" (NASB). As my husband and I began decreeing the Word of God over Merri, we watched in awe as a miraculous transformation began occurring slowly within her. Merri's mind and body were deteriorating at a rapid pace over the previous years. She had digressed to the point of not being able to complete a logical phrase when speaking. Her voice would trail off mid-sentence until she would sheepishly reply that she couldn't remember what she was going to say. She would often ask us for the phone number of one of our siblings, but when she would pick up the pencil to write it down, her hand would shake so badly that not a single number could be read. Her vision was failing and she was unable to even read a book.

Each time we visited Merri, we determined in our hearts that God was going to heal her just as He had healed me. We stopped listening to the reports of the doctors and began believing the report of the Lord. His report says that He died for Merri, took on all of her iniquities, and healed all of her diseases (Isaiah 53:4–5). We began speaking His promises over her life through daily phone calls, notes, and letters. We lived two and a half hours away but visited as often as we could to pray for her and speak life over her.

In just a few short months we began to see incredible improvements. Merri began reading her Bible. She began speaking God's Word over her own life. Soon she was able to write. She began filling up notebook after notebook with the most beautiful handwriting. I'll never forget the day she proudly called, excited to share that she had memorized her very first Bible verse: "Now faith is confidence in what we hope for and assurance about what we do not see" (Hebrews 11:1). As Merri began speaking this verse over her life, she was walking into it! This from a woman who had been diagnosed with early-onset Alzheimer's disease! The Lord was restoring to her everything the enemy had come in and stolen. We could not keep up with purchasing enough spiral-bound notebooks for her to write in. Eventually, one of Merri's siblings purchased a laptop for her. Within months she had completed a book which contains the story of her life. We are in utter amazement at the miracle that continues to take place in Merri's mind and body. We are convinced, without a doubt, that she will walk out of her care facility someday, fully healed and restored to the life she was destined to live.

Merri has started writing her second book, a book on healing. Only God could orchestrate this miracle that no doctor had even begun to imagine. God took her life, redeemed her from the plans of the enemy, and has given her new purpose and destiny. He restored her identity. She knows who she is—a child of the living God—and is now living her life from that truth. Even though she is still residing in a long-term care facility at the time of this writing, she is no longer living as the sick, mentally and physically ill victim that the devil tried to make her believe she was. She is living as a daughter of the King, full of authority and power.

Merri's testimony has given me a boldness to speak Scripture over everyone I know who is struggling. The verse "He sent out His Word and healed them; He rescued them from the grave" (Psalm 107:20) now becomes, "He sent out His Word and healed *Sue*; He rescued her from the grave." I insert names into the Scripture, believing it will come to pass for the person, and speaking it out loud over them. I am activating the power of decreeing the Word of God. God spoke the world into being. He opened His mouth and spoke, and whatever He spoke came to be. "In the beginning was the Word, and the Word was with God, and the Word was God" (John 1:1). God is the Word. When we speak the Word, we activate the power of God over lives.

## The Word is Your Weapon

I am convinced that we need to begin speaking the Word of God over every area of our lives that does not align with who God says we are and His plans for us. The enemy comes in and attempts to steal our destinies. We must rise up as the Ekklesia and fight back. Instead of pleading, "Please, God," like many of us do in our desperation, we must war with the authority we have been given as sons and daughters of the Lord God! Begin decreeing out loud, inserting your name or the name of your loved one into the Scriptures. "'For I know the plans I have for Merri,' declares the LORD, 'plans to prosper her and not to harm her, plans to give her hope and a future'" (Jeremiah 29:11, paraphrased).

Psalm 1:1–3 is one of my favorites that I pray almost daily over my husband:

> How blessed is my husband, Bill, who does not walk in the counsel of the wicked, nor stand in the path of sinners, nor sit in the seat of scoffers! But his delight is in the law of the LORD and in His law he meditates day and night. He will be like a tree *firmly* planted by streams of water, which yields its fruit in its season and its leaf does not wither, and in whatever he does, he prospers. (NASB; paraphrased)

I have prayed that Scripture over him for many years, and it has come to pass in his life. We must recognize and understand the *power* of the Word of God. Isaiah 55:11 promises, "So shall My Word be that goes forth out of My mouth: it shall not return unto Me void, but it shall accomplish that which I please, and it shall prosper in the thing for which I sent it" (King James 2000).

Decreeing the Word of God was another key strategy in my own healing testimony. The same brothers and sisters who were prophesying over me were also speaking the Word of God over my body and life. The Word was going out, accomplishing and prospering in the thing for which it was being sent. God's Word cannot be spoken and not do what it says it's going to do. That would be contrary to God's nature and character. He promised that His Word *would not* return void. I never understood the magnitude of this until people began speaking it over my life and my circumstances. As they spoke the Word of God over me, it came to fruition in my life!

This truth has opened up a whole new world to me. My mind has been transformed. My view of God has exploded! I knew He was so much bigger and greater than I could ever have imagined. I knew He could heal me. I knew He was a good Father, yet I never understood the power and magnitude of His Word, and I hadn't believed that He would heal *me*. All of a sudden, I was living it. As I began to partner and agree with the words being spoken over me, my heart was being healed from the inside out. As my heart was being healed, my illnesses began falling off one by one. I was a miracle in the making. You can read more of my healing testimony in my book *Smiling on the Outside, Dying on the Inside*.

It is pertinent that we contend with the enemy by using the sword of the Spirit, which is the Word of God. Many in the Body of Christ are a shadow of their potential because they are believing the lies of the devil. When Satan tempted Jesus in the wilderness for 40 days, Jesus used the Word of God to come against every lie the enemy threw at Him. He combated the lies with the truth found in His Word. We must have the Bible so engrained in us that when we open our mouths, the very oracles of God pour forth (1 Peter 4:11). We must eat the living scroll of God (Ezekiel 3:1–3), insert our names in the scroll, and watch the scroll come to pass everywhere we go.

Many people struggle with illness, addiction, depression, and loneliness, but God is a God of grace, mercy, and compassion. He already died for all of your struggles. All He asks is that you believe that what He accomplished on the cross was for you. If all you have strength to do is to say *yes* and sit in His presence, then do it! As you sit, unplug yourself from all outside stimuli. Turn off the television, social media, and other noise. Put your phone away and be still. You will begin to hear Him speak as you declutter your mind from the constant bombardment of sound. Ask Him to speak to you. He is waiting for you with anticipation. The Lord is calling His Ekklesia to a season of deep intimacy. Open your Bible. Meditate on His Word. The most prevalent way He speaks to us is through His written Word. Ask Him to teach you something new. Ask for fresh revelation! He is a good Father and He gives freely to those who ask. When I read the Word, I ask the Lord to supernaturally expand my brain capacity to be able to recall and put into action all I am reading.

He is pursuing His bride. He is taking us through a purifying process, making us ready. The process has been painful, but oh, the beauty that is yet to come! Diamonds are made from carbon that has been put through intense heat and pressure. Olive oil comes from an extreme pressing process. The reward comes from going through the fire, the pressure, the intensity. Allow God to take you through the pain because it is guaranteed that you will come out radiant!

## Miracle Testimony

A couple of years ago my friend Stuart DeVane was diagnosed with a hernia and was experiencing severe pain. He has allowed me to share with you his testimony in his own words. You will be encouraged when you read his miraculous story:

> During the fall of 2018 I was diagnosed by my physician's assistant as having a hernia. An ultrasound revealed what appeared to be a large black hole. I asked the technician if there was any way the hernia could be sewed up without a mesh, and she replied there was no possible way to sew it up. Preparation began by consulting a surgeon who concurred that a mesh could be sewn from the outside or inside the hernia, but there was no way a mesh could be

avoided. I had read numerous reports of people having complications from the mesh after hernia surgery and was hoping to avoid having to have a mesh placed in my body.

At this point I contacted people to pray for me. Bill and Debbie Bilek prayed for me face-to-face every week for 6 weeks, anointing me with oil, laying hands on me, speaking many healing Scriptures over me, and encouraging me.

On my surgery date, the surgeon shared that the procedure would require an hour or more to complete. My wife was surprised to see the surgeon after only 20 minutes. When I awoke the surgeon said he found no hernia, that no mesh was needed, and that he had glued the incision he made back together!

That, my friends, is the power of the Word of God! When we speak it out, it has to come to pass. Bill and I were not the only ones praying for Stuart, and we know without a doubt that God heard the many prayers going up on his behalf and healed him.

Begin speaking the Word of God over your life, your family, your circumstances, your region, your state, your country, and the world. Watch God move as He awakens your heart for the bigger picture. You are not here to just survive. You are here to thrive and live a powerful life of influence. You are destined to be a world changer. God spoke the world into being. Begin to speak to your mountains and they will be moved! "Truly I tell you, if anyone says to this mountain, 'Go, throw yourself into the

*We need to begin speaking the Word of God over every area of our lives that does not align with who God says we are and His plans for us.*

sea,' and does not doubt in their heart but believes that what they say will happen, it will be done for them. Therefore I tell you, whatever you ask for in prayer, believe that you have received it, and it will be yours" (Mark 11:23–24). I hear the Lord saying that His people are only a portion of their potential because they are believing the lies. It's time to silence the voice of the enemy and activate the voice of God!

Lord, I pray that You awaken Your bride. Awaken Your Ekklesia to the power of speaking the Word of God. Thank You that Your Word is living and active, sharper than a double-edged sword and that it penetrates even to the dividing of soul and spirit, joints and marrow. Thank You that it judges the thoughts and attitudes of the heart (Hebrews 4:12). When we open our mouths let us speak the very oracles of God (1 Peter 4:11) that we may watch our words become Your Words and align with Your heart and plans for this next season. In the mighty name that is above every other name, Jesus Christ our Lord. Amen.

## CHAPTER 3

# Worship

*Come, let us sing for joy to the LORD;*
*Let us shout aloud to the Rock of our salvation.*

*Psalm 95:1*

One day while feeling down in the dumps about a decision someone very close to me was making, I made the conscious effort to quit moping around and to get on with my life. After all, I had absolutely zero control over this person or the decision being made. I was in a real slump and needed to pull myself out. I decided to turn on some worship music and start cleaning up the house to get my mind off of what I couldn't change or fix. The music began to instantly bless my soul as the words to the song "Defender" filled the room.

You go before I know
That You've even gone to win my war.
And You come back with the head of my enemy,
You come back and You call it my victory.

All I did was praise.
All I did was worship.
All I did was bow down.
All I did was stay still.

Hallelujah, You have saved me.
It's so much better this way.
Hallelujah, great defender.
It's so much better Your way.

When I thought I lost me, You knew where I left me.
You reintroduced me to Your love.
You picked up all my pieces, You put me back together,
You are the defender of my heart.[1]

Soon I was actually dancing around the kitchen putting dishes away, while singing out loud. This song says it all. When I choose to praise and worship, God goes to war to defend me. He is the defender of my heart.

The next song began to play. The words, "This is how I fight my battles," rang through the air over and over as I began singing "Surrounded" by Michael W. Smith.[2] I sang out at the top of my lungs, "It may look like I'm surrounded, but I'm surrounded by You." All of a sudden I heard a loud crash in the next room. I raced in and found a picture of a dragon-headed snake smack-dab in the middle of the floor. I thought to myself, *That's really strange. Where did that come from?* I texted my daughter, who was away at college, and asked her about the painting. She reminded me she had painted it several years earlier as a required assignment for an art class.

The assignment was to copy the image of a book cover that displayed this Chinese dragon that was now lying in the middle of the room. She said it had been hanging on a nail behind her bedroom door for a couple of years.

I sat there in confusion. Moments earlier I had been in her room to fill the dog's water dish, and there was nothing in the middle of the floor. Now this painting was lying there. If it had been hanging *behind* an open door, how did it jump off of the nail and land over in the middle of the room? An eerie feeling began to rise up in my spirit. I decided to talk to God about it. As I asked Him to calm my heart and mind and clue me in to what had taken place, I felt Him showing me the power of our worship.

The painting that had jumped off of the wall, and landed in the middle of the room demonstrated to me that the enemy cannot stand to hear our worship and praise! This dragon-headed serpent represented the enemy. The Bible, in the book of Genesis, refers to Satan as a serpent. Revelation 12:9 states, "The great dragon was hurled down—that ancient serpent called the devil, or Satan, who leads the whole world astray." In that moment, the Lord revealed to me the power of our worship. When we worship God, He goes to war for us and all darkness has to flee—or in this case, jump off the wall and bow to the King of kings. The enemy cannot stand to hear the name of Jesus.

> When we worship God, He goes to war for us and all darkness has to flee.

## *Weapon of Warfare*

As a person begins to worship, his whole demeanor shifts. Worship and praise push back darkness. The enemy has to run! Satan and his cohorts cannot stand to hear the sound of worship to our God. It is a powerful weapon of warfare.

When I am feeling down or the thoughts of the enemy creep in to taunt me, I crank up the volume and worship.

> Therefore, I urge you, brothers and sisters, in view of God's mercy, to offer your bodies as a living sacrifice, holy and pleasing to God—*this is your true and proper worship*. Do not conform to the pattern of this world, but be transformed by the renewing of your mind. Then you will be able to test and approve what God's will is— His good, pleasing and perfect will. (Romans 12:1–2; emphasis mine)

When we sing praise to God, it shifts something in our own mind *and* in the spiritual realm. It is an act of worship, pleasing to God. It transforms us.

Corporate worship is even more powerful! It has the ability to pull down strongholds and transform regions and even nations. I absolutely love the story in 2 Chronicles 20, where the king of Judah was in despair. He and his people were surrounded on all sides by several other nations. It looked pretty grim. There seemed to be no escape. King Jehoshaphat called the people to fast, pray, and seek the Lord. The Lord answered them and said, "Do not be afraid or discouraged because of this vast multitude, for the battle is not yours, but God's" (2 Chronicles 20:15, HCSB). They were given encouragement and strategy. Jehoshaphat told the people to believe in the Lord their God:

> Then he consulted with the people and *appointed some to sing for the LORD and some to praise the splendor of His holiness*. When they went out in front of the armed forces, they kept singing: "Give thanks to the LORD, for His faithful love endures forever." The moment they began their shouts and praises, the LORD set an ambush against the Ammonites, Moabites, and the inhabitants of Mount Seir who came to fight against Judah, and

they were defeated. (2 Chronicles 20:21–22, HCSB; emphasis mine)

This is such awesome revelation! They sent the worshippers out first, on the front lines, *in front of* the armed forces! When they began their shouts and songs of praise, the Lord moved in and defeated the enemies on all sides. The soldiers never even had to lift a finger or a weapon to fight! Their worship was their weapon of war! All they did was sing songs of praise to the Lord. Then *He* turned the enemies on themselves, and *all* of the enemies were defeated.

## Worship Through the Difficult Seasons

When my youngest daughter was in high school, she experienced a period of being tormented at night by fear. As the Lord gave revelation, she downloaded hours and hours of worship music onto her iPod (remember those?) and played it all night long. Whenever she had the worship music playing, she did not wake up with nightmares, fear, or torment. She ended up sleeping with worship music playing through the night for several years. This was another real-life demonstration as to how powerful the weapon of worship is.

As we go through difficult seasons, we must sing praise to the King. If you are like me, sometimes I feel such an intensity from the attack that I get overwhelmed. It is imperative during those times that I implement this strategy to pull myself out of the slump. Begin the shift! Know that your praise and worship does not fall on deaf ears. The Lord loves a heart of worship! Begin singing Scripture over your lives, over your family, over your region, and over your nation. It will shift everything! The war in the heavenlies will begin as the angel armies rush in to fight on your behalf.

I love to sing through the book of Psalms. I open to a passage and begin to sing it out loud. It pulls me right up out of the heaviness. When something happens that causes me to feel down or distracted, I find an appropriate Scripture and begin to sing it out. This strategy lifts me from stress and worry into the peace of the God of the universe!

We can cry, pout, and live in fear and anxiety over our present circumstances and the chaos around the world that we read about in the news and see on television… Or we can choose to worship and praise the King of kings and Lord of lords while watching Him dive in to redeem the situation in His perfect timing. "When the enemy shall come in like a flood, the Spirit of the LORD shall lift up a standard against him" (Isaiah 59:19, KJV).

Sing this passage aloud with me as we worship the Lord and watch Him raise up a standard against the enemy over His Ekklesia!

> Hallelujah! Praise the Lord! Let the skies be filled with praise
> and the highest heavens with the shouts of glory!
> Go ahead—praise Him, all you His messengers!
> Praise Him some more, all you heavenly hosts!
> Keep it up, sun and moon!
> Don't stop now, all you twinkling stars of light!
> Take it up even higher—up to the highest heavens,
> until the cosmic chorus thunders His praise!
> Let the entire universe erupt with praise to God.
> From nothing to something He spoke and created it all.
> He established the cosmos to last forever,
> and He stands behind His commands
> so His orders will never be revoked.
> Let the earth join in with this parade of praise!
> You mighty creatures of the ocean's depths,
> echo in exaltation!
> Lightning, hail, snow, and clouds,
> and the stormy winds that fulfill His Word.

Bring your melody, O mountains and hills;
trees of the forest and field, harmonize your praise!
Praise Him, all beasts and birds, mice and men,
kings, queens, princes, and princesses,
young men and maidens, children and babes,
old and young alike, everyone everywhere!
Let them all join in with this orchestra of praise.
For the name of the Lord is the only name we raise!
His stunning splendor ascends higher than the heavens.
He anoints His people with strength and authority,
showing His great favor to all His godly lovers,
even to His princely people, Israel,
who are so close to His heart.
Hallelujah! Praise the Lord! (Psalm 148 TPT)

CHAPTER 4

# *Pray*

*The prayer of a righteous person is powerful and effective.*

James 5:16

A couple of years ago I participated in a ten-day prayer gathering where hundreds of people came together to cry out for revival in our region, our state, our nation, and the world. It was a strategic time as believers from around the globe united in love and purpose. At one point during the conference, we received news that the United States of America had decided to engage in the war in Syria. The conference facilitator called one of my friends up on stage to pray over that region. My friend, who is from the Middle East, began praying in her native tongue. We all felt the tangible presence of the Holy Spirit fall on the room. She then began screaming out in English, with urgency, to the lost and the unsaved in that region. She was shouting, "There is a God who loves you! We call you in! We pull you in! We call you in! We pull you in!" It was a powerful moment in time, and I am getting Holy Spirit goosebumps as I type these words and relive the memories of that experience.

The next morning the Lord woke me at 2:30 a.m. He showed me a vision of what happened at that moment in time as five hundred people in a small city on the Central Coast of California came together to pray. As the Lord brought to memory the evening prayer, He began to pull back the veil and show me what was happening in the spirit realm. I saw my friend on the stage praying in her native tongue. As she prayed, fiery arrows were being launched out of her mouth, heading straight at the bombs that had been released over Syria. The bombs were being intercepted before they hit the ground! Then I saw thousands of civilians on the ground looking up at the bombs coming their way, sheer terror on their faces! As my friend began shouting about a God who loves them and repeating over and over "We call you in! We pull you in," I saw the people on the ground, both hands in the air, raised to heaven, screaming out, "*Jesus, save us!*"

Later that morning I couldn't wait to read the news reports to see what had happened. I looked up a Middle Eastern news source and found that a significant number of the launched bombs had been intercepted before hitting the ground![1] That, my friends, is the power of prayer! And I know in my spirit that thousands had cried out to Jesus to save them that day.

## Keys of the Kingdom

Do you wonder if God really hears you *every* time you pray? If He is truly all knowing, then do you really need to voice what you are feeling, thinking, or needing? God is a personal God who longs for deep intimacy with His creation. Oftentimes in life we succumb to feelings of helplessness. I have heard

> *"...whatever you bind on earth will be bound in heaven, and whatever you loose on earth will be loosed in heaven."*

many well-meaning believers say, "All we can do is pray." That never bothered me, until the Lord began showing me what we are actually doing when we pray. When we open our mouths to pray, we have the power to bind and loose things on earth. Matthew 16:19 boasts, "I will give you the keys of the Kingdom of Heaven; whatever you bind on earth will be bound in heaven, and whatever you loose on earth will be loosed in heaven." This is amazing to comprehend. When I call it forth on earth, it happens in heaven. Now instead of saying, "All I can do is pray," I say, "Yay! Something else I get to pray about!" We should be praying *before* we do anything else, instead of trying everything else first. We have no power to fix or change our circumstances, but God has *all* power and has given us the keys to the Kingdom. What an awesome privilege to be able to partner with God and His heavenly host to shift atmospheres, transform lives, usher in healing and deliverance, and to call forth what is not as if it were and watch it become (Romans 4:17, King James 2000).

Have you ever heard the saying, "If you can see it, you can have it"? This is such a divine concept. The Lord gives us dreams and visions for the purpose of visualizing what He has for us in the future so we can pull it into the present. This may be hard to wrap our heads around, but it is truth. As we read in an earlier chapter, Hebrews 11:1 says, "Now faith is confidence in what we hope for and assurance about what we do not see." We need to ask God to show us our circumstances from heaven's viewpoint. Jesus died for our sins and for our iniquities. His blood covered all. We must ask the Lord to help us see ourselves, other people, and global situations that we pray for from His perspective. Then we can align our prayers with heaven. This is powerful stuff!

God has given me the revelation that before I pray for someone, I need to get His heart for the individual—to see the person through His eyes. We all have our earthly perspective and view of people. We come to conclusions based on the looks or behaviors of any given individual. We must switch this to asking God to allow us to see people through His eyes. This has shifted everything for me. I know that every person is born with purpose and with a destiny to fulfill on this earth. Each one is precious in His sight no matter the choices they have made or the circumstances they may find themselves in. When we view a person through heaven's lense, we are filled with compassion. There are numerous verses in the Bible that speak of Jesus being moved by compassion, healing those who were in need. Let's start operating and praying in the belief that when we pray with the heart of God, we are moving Him to act on behalf of the people and situations we are praying for.

## Never Give Up!

My husband has a friend whom we have known for over thirty years. This friend was not a kind man. For many years he went around doing as he pleased, saying whatever he felt like saying whenever he felt like saying it. Along life's road, he hurt and offended many people including his employees, customers, family members, neighbors, and anyone else who crossed his path. This man was married to a God-fearing woman who prayed for him each and every day, thinking he might never change, but not really wanting a divorce. Her days were filled with pain and anguish being married to such a cruel individual. One Sunday morning as she was getting ready for church, she noticed that her husband was showered, groomed, and dressed. She asked, "Where are you going?" He replied with a smile, "To church with you!" She about passed out. In their fourteen years of marriage, he had never once gone to church with her.

I tell you this story to encourage you to *never* quit praying for those you love. This man, in my husband's words, was the "least likely" candidate for change. The drastic shift in this friend's life came that Sunday morning as he accompanied his wife to church and heard the Gospel of Jesus Christ preached for the first time. The words penetrated to the depths of his soul. He went home pondering the transformative power of Jesus. Something in him had been shifted forever. Later that week he found himself in the pastor's office asking to be baptized, but the story doesn't end there! This man spent the next year going around to every person he could find that he had been unkind to, offended, or treated unfairly. He asked forgiveness of each one and left a trail of amazement everywhere he went. He joined the men's group at church and within two years had become a powerful leader in his church. My husband and I were in awe of the miraculous transformation in this friend that occurred almost overnight.

Never, never give up. Never stop praying no matter how grim the situation looks. God still does instant miracles. We have seen immediate healings and lives transformed instantly. We have read about entire communities coming to Jesus. That is the power of prayer. God hears from heaven, sends angels into action to partner with those prayers, and moves mountains on our behalf. Hebrews 1:14 reminds us, "Are not all angels ministering spirits sent to serve those who will inherit salvation?" Open your mouth to activate the angels. They are waiting for their assignment, and we see that they are activated at the voice of His Word. "Praise the LORD, you His angels, you mighty ones who do His bidding, who obey His Word" (Psalm 103:20).

The Bible is loaded with prayers of faith, prayers of agreement, prayers of request, prayers of thanksgiving, prayers of worship, prayers of dedication, prayers of intercession, and praying in the Spirit. There is no right or wrong way to pray. It is more an attitude of the heart. In other words, you can't get it wrong.

I had a friend who used to sit at her kitchen table each morning with two cups of coffee. She had a chair and a cup of coffee for herself and another one for Jesus. She started each day with her chair facing the seemingly empty chair. In reality, the chair wasn't empty at all! She was sitting and talking with her Lord in a most intimate exchange. God just wants to chat with us. He longs for that personal quality time with His Ekklesia. Today, let's choose to sit in His presence and meditate on what it really means to *pray without ceasing* (1 Thessalonians 5:17, ESV). Discover true intimacy in prayer as you pour out your heart to a loving, personal God who longs to hear your voice. This is an integral strategy to come against the harassing powers of darkness. Let's begin praying as Jesus did. "Your Kingdom come, Your will be done, on earth as it is in heaven" (Matthew 6:10). Let's partner with Jesus in bringing heaven to earth.

## Pray it Right

Whatever you see that is wrong or out of alignment with the Word of God is an opportunity for you to step in and pray it right. Remember that God has put you there to flip it:

- Instead of praying, "Oh God, fix my wife," pray, "Thank You, God, that You are molding and shaping my wife into the mighty woman of God that You have destined her to be."

- Instead of praying, "Lord, I need more money to pay the bills and make ends meet," pray, "Thank You, God, that I am a child of the King and that You are my provider who meets my every need. I decree that in my household there will be no lack. Thank You that we have more than enough to pay all of our bills with an abundant overflow to bless the poor and needy in our midst. Thank You that my family is being used as a funnel of resources to bless the nations."

- Instead of praying, "God, heal my body," pray, "Thank You, God, that You heal all of my diseases, that You took all of my pain and suffering when You died on the cross."

- Instead of going to an addiction recovery meeting and declaring, "Hello my name is _____ and I am an alcoholic," decree, "My name is _____ and I am a child of the King. I was created in His image. I am covered by His blood. By His stripes I am healed. Thank You, Lord, that I have been freed from all bondages of addiction and sin, and that in Christ I am a new creation. I have the mind of Christ. As I seek first the Kingdom of God and His righteousness, all these things will be added unto me" (Matthew 6:33, King James 2000).

- Instead of praying, "Oh God, help my nation," pray with the power and authority given to you through Jesus Christ, "The United States of America (or whatever nation you are from) shall be saved!"

Pray with me:

Lord, let us become a people of prayer, a people who move mountains, a people who pull down strongholds, lies, and every high thing that exalts itself against the knowledge of You (2 Corinthians 10:4–5, AKJV). Let us pray with the faith of a mustard seed and trust that as we pray, You and Your angelic heavenly host are orchestrating things on behalf of Your children. God, Your heart is *for* us, not against us. We know Your will is that we walk in Your ways all the days of our lives. We know that as the prayers of the Ekklesia align with Your will, they have to come to pass. Thank You that

You love us and that Your heart is to heal us and set us free to become overflowing vessels of Your love and power. We lay our lives before Your throne and say thank You, God, that You redeemed us from the grasp of the enemy when You died on the cross. Help us to see ourselves as rectified, redeemed, and restored that we may step into Your reality for our lives. Use us for Your glory, Lord, as we pray right that which is wrong. In Jesus' name. Amen.

CHAPTER 5

# Pray in the Spirit

*And pray in the Spirit on all occasions with
all kinds of prayers and requests.*

Ephesians 6:18

Praying in the Spirit is a powerful weapon of war. I remember the day I prayed in the Spirit (in tongues) for the first time. I had been asking the Lord for the baptism of the Holy Spirit with the evidence of tongues that I had read about in the book of Acts. I did not understand it, nor did I fully believe He would give it to me. I think deep down part of me was afraid of it. I had seen "those" people and the way they acted at times. I had witnessed them laughing hysterically, shrieking, shaking, falling to the ground, groaning uncontrollably, crying, and outright causing a scene! I was very comfortable being in control of my behavior and actions. Did I really want to let go and let God? I was a prideful person who cared about what others thought of me and who always tried to make a good impression. Growing up in a conservative, mainstream denomination, I was not introduced to praying in the Spirit, or in tongues, until much later in life. I am still being challenged daily with what it means to "Pray in the Spirit on *all occasions* with all kinds of prayers and requests" (Ephesians 6:18, emphasis mine).

As I began to hunger and thirst for more of God, I found myself going up to the altar at conferences and church services when they would offer to pray for anyone wanting the baptism of the Holy Spirit. I felt humiliated time and time again as they prayed for me. Some would gently touch me on my head or give me a little shove, expecting me to fall over. Some would tell me to just open my mouth and say, "dadadadada" or "babababa." "It will come," they assured me. To my shame and embarrassment, it never did. I became more and more intimidated and sank deeper into the belief that God did not want to share this gift with me. I began thinking it was only for *some* people, *special* people.

One day my dear friend, Pastor Hudson Suubi, from Uganda, was visiting. He was preaching at my church about the glory and the anointing that come with the baptism of the Holy Spirit. He shared his testimony of how before he was baptized in the Holy Spirit, he would cling to his notes when preaching the Word of God. Knowing him personally and having seen him boldly preach the Word of God on numerous occasions, always *without* notes, I could not imagine a time this man ever needed notes! I wanted what he had! So, there I found myself the following week in a prayer room with two strangers, fifty miles from home, confessing to them that I wanted to be baptized in the Holy Spirit. They were the sweetest elderly couple and told me not to worry about it, that I didn't need to strive or beg or struggle for it. They prayed for me and reassured me that God would give me this gift freely at a time when I least expected it.

On my hour drive home, I opened my mouth to pray and out came the strangest words. It sounded like a foreign dialect from some hidden tribe unknown to mankind. I was totally caught off guard. It sounded so funny. I thought, *Really, God? Is this what speaking in tongues is? Does it have to sound so strange?* You'd think I would have been elated to have finally received this precious heavenly language. But instead, I found myself complaining to God about how it sounded! As I was around other Spirit-filled believers, I began listening to them as they prayed in tongues. It always sounded so beautiful, so eloquent, so heavenly. I was self-conscious to pray in the Spirit out loud. I am a tad embarrassed to even be mentioning this right now and don't know why I am, but I believe it will minister to someone reading this. I soon became a closet pray-er. I only prayed in tongues in the privacy of my own home, when no one else was around.

God is such a gracious, patient, loving Father. He must have been cracking up at me! I am laughing right now as I think about how I wanted a gift, asked and pleaded for the gift, finally got the gift, and then was uncomfortable in using the gift. The Lord was quietly and patiently teaching me humility. I had always been concerned with what others thought of me to the point of wanting to choose the sound that would come out of my mouth while praying in the Spirit. Oh, what a mess I was! God was molding me and shaping me into the person He had created me to be as I was being knit together in my mother's womb. He is so gracious to take our brokenness and make beauty from our ashes.

As I began "closet" praying in the Spirit, God began doing a miraculous work from the inside out. Romans 8:26 states, "…the Spirit helps us in our weakness. We do not know what we ought to pray for, but the Spirit himself intercedes for us through wordless groans." My "groanings," though pretty funny sounding, were actually God making intercession for me! I look back and thank God for His patience, lovingkindness, and intercession. I was ungrateful, disrespectful, and arrogant, yet He still chose to make intercession for me. That is the beautiful heart of the Father toward His wayward children.

## It's a Partnership

Roger Williams, Senior Pastor of CrossRoads Church in Atascadero, California explains praying in the Spirit like this:

> I heard many years ago that language is an agreement between two or more people that the sounds you make have meaning. For example, the word and sound "chair" does not have the same meaning in non-English speaking countries as it does with us. We have made an agreement as to what "chair" means. Praying in the Spirit is quite similar in that it is an agreement with God that the sounds you make have meaning. So, praying in tongues is a faith agreement between you and the Lord, a step of faith which, of course, requires participation, just as with every other gift of the Holy Spirit.

*To think that when I pray in the Spirit, I am partnering with Almighty God to bring heaven to earth!*

In other words, we have to open our mouths and choose to make the sound. I thank God for His gentleness with me. I have seen His miraculous intervention in my life through praying in the Spirit. I am a different person than I was before being baptized in the Holy Spirit. I praise Him for His patience, partnership, intervention, and wisdom. I am convinced that we should be praying in the Spirit as much as we can. It is one thing for me to pray with my human mind, but to think that the God of the universe is making intercession for me is incomprehensible! To know that when I pray in the Spirit, I am partnering with Almighty God to bring heaven to earth is mind blowing!

When I picture what took place in the book of Acts, I can't help but shout!

> When the day of Pentecost came, they were all together in one place. Suddenly a sound like the blowing of a violent wind came from heaven and filled the whole house where they were sitting. They saw what seemed to be tongues of fire that separated and came to rest on each of them. All of them were filled with the Holy Spirit and began to speak in other tongues as the Spirit enabled them. (Acts 2:1–4)

This experience in the upper room transformed them forever! Before they were filled with the Holy Spirit, they were huddled together in fear, hiding out, praying in the upper room behind locked doors. After they were baptized in the Holy Spirit everything changed!

Jesus had promised earlier in Acts 1:8, "But you will receive *power* when the Holy Spirit comes on you; and you will be My witnesses in Jerusalem, and in all Judea and Samaria, and to the ends of the earth" (emphasis mine). All of a sudden, things shifted! After receiving the Holy Spirit, weak, cowardly Peter, who had denied the Lord three times due to fear, was transformed into a strong, *bold* preacher of the Gospel. The people who heard Peter speak were astonished at his boldness. How could Peter, an uneducated fisherman, speak with such power and authority? He was no longer afraid of persecution! People saw the transformation in him. This ordinary disciple became an extraordinary man of God:

> When they saw the courage of Peter and John and realized that they were unschooled, ordinary men, they

were astonished and they took note that these men had been with Jesus. (Acts 4:13)

This is the power of the baptism of the Holy Spirit and praying in tongues. When we don't know what to pray with our human minds, the Holy Spirit intercedes for us! What a concept! When I am in despair over my health, my finances, or the choices my loved ones are making… when I am overwhelmed by political, governmental, economic and world crises that seem hopeless… when everything in the universe seems to be spinning out of control, God knows exactly what needs to happen and partners with me to pray things right.

At this point you may be questioning the difference between the gift of tongues and praying in the Spirit. There is much to study and consider on this topic, but a simple explanation is that the gift of tongues refers to speaking in tongues for the edification of the Body of Christ, in other words, to encourage the church. We find this gift cited in 1 Corinthians 14 where Paul discusses the gifts of the Spirit. Used in this manner, we see that tongues must be followed by interpretation, in order to build up the entire church. This is a gift imparted by God to those He chooses.

On the other hand, praying in the Spirit is something made available to everyone at all times. It does not require interpretation because it is a language given for your personal use to build you up in your spirit. Ephesians 6:18 says, "And pray in the Spirit on all occasions with all kinds of prayers and requests." As we discussed earlier in Romans 8:26, praying in the Spirit is actually the Spirit of God making intercession for us when we don't know what or how to pray.

## *This is Somebody's Son*

Last year I attended a church service where Ashley Little, founder of *Greater Love Ministries*, was sharing her testimony of how the Lord had saved her out of a lifestyle of drug and alcohol addiction and homosexuality. During worship, I noticed a young man behind me who was bent over and crying. I went over to him and asked if I could pray for him. As I reached out to place my hand on his shoulder, he fell into me and began sobbing uncontrollably. He wreaked of alcohol, and I could tell he was strung out on something. I stood there holding him in my arms, just hugging him and praying. He kept sobbing and began to cry out, "It's too hard! It's too hard!" I silently asked the Lord to give me His heart for this young man. Immediately, a picture of my dear friend's son, who was severely addicted to drugs, passed before my eyes. I embraced this stranger even tighter as the Lord showed me my friend's son—the young man I had been fervently praying for over the past couple of years. All I could think about was my beloved friend and her son as the Lord quietly whispered to me, "This is somebody's son."

I was at a loss as to how to help this individual, so I began praying in tongues. I knew that the God of heaven was looking down at this broken young man who had walked into that service off of the street. I knew in that moment I was involved in a divine appointment that the Lord had orchestrated. He placed me there to demonstrate the tangible love of Jesus. I was Jesus' hands and feet in action, speaking life and love into a broken young man. He was encountering Jesus as I held him and partnered with God in prayer. I know that his life will never be the same.

In Smith Wigglesworth's devotional book, he writes:

> If I were to come to you right now and say, "Whatever you do, you must try to be holy," I would miss it. I would be altogether outside of God's plan. But I take the words of the epistle, which says by the Holy Spirit, "Be holy" (1 Peter 1:16). It is easy as possible to be holy, but you can never be holy by your own efforts. God wants us to

be entirely eaten up by this holy zeal for Him, so that every day we will walk in the Spirit. It is lovely to walk in the Spirit, for He will cause you to dwell in safety, to rejoice inwardly, and to praise God reverently.[1]

I believe that so many individuals who have given their lives to Jesus fail and fall prey to the same self-destructive behaviors over and over again because they are trying to get it right in their own power. This is where the baptism of the Holy Spirit comes in. We cannot be holy or strive to live a life of righteousness in our own carnal flesh. We will fail over and over again. This is why much of the church looks as sick as the rest of the world. We have strived to do it on our own. By our own strength we cannot possibly overcome the attacks of Satan over our marriages, families, bodies, minds, finances, communities, and every other way he comes after us. Once we have received the baptism of the Holy Spirit, with the evidence of tongues, it is crucial to begin praying in the Spirit on all occasions. In this way we are continually building ourselves up as the Lord Himself intercedes for us.

Do you want the mind of Christ? Do you want to open your mouth and speak His words? Do you want to be able to control your tongue, your attitude, and your actions? Then you must pray in tongues. James 3:8 states, "but no human being can tame the tongue. It is a restless evil, full of deadly poison." The only way to tame the tongue is by praying in the Spirit. How many of you are like me, lashing out when angered, or saying something we wish we could take back? As we pray in the Spirit, we become engrained with His mind. The more we pray in the Spirit, the more we become like Christ, being built up with His thoughts, His words, and His ways. We receive breakthrough so that when we open our mouths, we speak the very oracles of God (1 Peter 4:11). When we pray in tongues, we receive the heart of God and we put angels on assignment!

## Pray in the Spirit

I challenge you to begin praying in the Spirit first thing when you get up in the morning, when you take a shower, when you drive to work, and every chance you get. This will keep your mind focused on the right perspective for the entire course of your day. Praying in tongues builds us up in our inner man. I often pray in tongues when my mind begins to wander or attempts to take me to a bad place. As I pray, the Lord immediately gives me His mindset and pulls me right out of the pit I was going down. Praying this way aligns us with what the Father is doing. Let's be about His business and not waste any more time trying to get it right on our own. We cannot fail when God is advocating on our behalf.

Pray with me:

Holy Spirit, teach Your Ekklesia to partner with You in prayer. Teach us what it truly means to pray in the Spirit at all times. I am in awe of what You are doing in the spiritual realm as we take time to partner with You. Thank You that You love us so much that You intercede for us. Thank You for showing us that there is nothing more important we can be doing with our time than to be spending it with You. We can be out there "doing," or we can be resting in Your presence, allowing *You* to do what You do best. Have Your way in each of us. Show us what it looks like to partner with You in prayer, allowing You to be God over our seemingly impossible situations. Remind us that nothing is impossible with You. In Jesus' name we pray. Amen.

If anyone reading this has not yet been baptized in the Holy Spirit and received your personal prayer language, I would like to pray for you now. This is an opportunity to receive the power and boldness that came to the apostles in the upper room. This will change your life. No longer will you strive in the flesh to get it right. God will begin to work in and through you with the anointing He will impart from heaven. It will become second nature to live a supernatural life of righteousness, peace, and joy.

Please hold your hands out in a posture to receive:

> Lord God, I pray for the ones reading these words right now to receive Your gift of the baptism of the Holy Spirit. As You did for me, please do for them to an even greater degree of anointing. As they open their mouths right now, fill them with Your heavenly language and give them a personal encounter with the Living God. Thank You that You are Lord. Thank You that You intercede for us with heavenly groanings. Thank You that You do not leave us alone to fend for ourselves when we know not how to pray. Thank You that You are God and we are not. We release all of our burdens to You, and we take Your yoke, for Your yoke is easy and Your burden is light (Matthew 11:30). Thank You that You are who You say You are, and that You do what You say You do. In Jesus' name we pray. Amen.

CHAPTER 6

# *Give Thanks*

*Give thanks in all circumstances...*

*1 Thessalonians 5:18*

I turned the corner to the waiting room to await my turn for an MRI of my injured knee. It was as if I had entered the twilight zone. My heart stopped for a moment as I saw a room full of people all dressed the same. Each one had on a matching hospital gown, white with a pale blue design, complimented by light blue pajama pants. As I glanced at the stone-cold faces, I could see fear and death written on each one. I caught my breath as the memory of a movie I had seen many years ago, *The Boy in the Striped Pajamas,*[1] came to mind. It was the story of a boy living in a concentration camp during the Holocaust. The scene flashing through my mind was when all of the people were wearing matching pajama-like uniforms, fear all over their faces. They were being led into a large room, herded like cattle, not knowing or understanding what was ahead of them. As the scene unfolded, the viewers began to understand that these people, all wearing the same uniform, had just entered the gas chambers and were facing certain death.

As I walked further into the waiting room, I plopped myself down onto the one vacant chair between two complete strangers. I glanced at each face in the room. Not one would make eye contact with me. I sat in silence asking God, *Why am I here?* I knew He had the power to heal me and that with just a spoken word it would happen. It was not a lack of faith. My faith was through the roof as I had personally experienced numerous miracles over the past several years in my own life and the lives of others. In my frustration, I decided to thank Him. I thanked Him that it was only an injured knee. Many were there awaiting their cancer diagnosis or death sentence. I thanked God that I had great medical insurance and would only have to pay a portion of the cost of the MRI. I thanked God that I was not alone, that He was with me. As more and more gratitude began welling up in my heart, I realized that I really wasn't there for my knee, I was there on assignment. A man came in, called out my name, then took me into a small changing room adjacent to the waiting room. I was issued my "uniform" and was told to put it on and then sit in a chair and wait my turn. As I sat back down, I determined in my heart that not one other person would walk into that room and feel the distress I had felt minutes earlier.

A while later, an elderly woman came around the corner. I saw the fear well up in her eyes as she looked at each of us wearing our uniform of death. I quickly blurted out, "Welcome to the party! Don't worry, soon you, too, will get your costume!" Everyone in the room broke out in laughter. All faces of stone were instantly wearing smiles. In one moment, the entire atmosphere of fear and death had shifted. A few minutes later, a father carrying a tiny boy in his arms rounded the corner. I saw the fear on the little boy's face. I noticed he was wearing his own green Ninja Turtle pajamas. I said, "Hey! Where did you get your pajamas? I want a pair like that! How come you got the cool pajamas and we all got these?" His face turned from fear into a proud smile. Others in the room began commenting on his pajamas. Soon the entire room was engaged in conversation with each other. People were laughing and smiling. I watched in amazement as fear left and peace and joy flooded in.

That, my friends, is the power of what we as believers carry. I didn't preach a sermon. I didn't pull out the four spiritual laws and begin reciting them while passing out tracts. I simply took the negative feeling of fear that I was experiencing and handed it to God. He took it, gave me my assignment, and then I acted on it. It's that simple. If we are truly the temple of the Holy Spirit (1 Corinthians 6:19) and we carry His presence everywhere we go, we should be shifting atmospheres of death and fear and be ushering in peace and joy.

Upon reflection, I wish I had taken it a step further. If I could return to that moment, I would ask for the boldness to begin laying hands on each person and praying for their healing. I wish I would have had the faith to bring forth what Christ did on the cross and watch it manifest in that room. It was no accident that I was in that room at that moment to penetrate the fear with the presence of God, who is also the healer.

May the Lord grant us the boldness and the anointing to usher in the fullness of His promises everywhere His Ekklesia sets foot. May we bring healing, deliverance, joy, peace, love, and the Kingdom of God everywhere we go.

## *Thankful in the Trials*

You might be asking, "How can I be thankful at a time like this?" I get it! When we turn on the news or simply look at the culture around us, we see evil in every realm of life. Negative emotions surge to the forefront before we even have time to think! Feelings of helplessness and hopelessness arise. I am here to tell you that is a lie of the enemy—a huge scheme of the devil to get you feeling so bad that you shut down and throw your hands in the air. That is exactly where Satan wants you—groveling, sulking, and giving up.

Personally, I spent far too many years focused on my illnesses rather than living life and giving thanks for what I did have. As each new diagnosis came, I would get on the internet, research it, make note of all the possible complications and side effects, and walk further and further into each one. I would partner with it in my mind and then spend all of my energy and money on it.

The heavenly strategy is the exact opposite. I thank God for the trials and tribulations around me. 1 Chronicles 16:34 reminds us to "Give thanks to the LORD, for He is good; His love endures forever." Do I believe He is good? Do I trust that His love endures forever? Yes! Then I choose to give thanks. Paul stated in 1 Thessalonians 5:18, "Give thanks in all circumstances; for this is God's will for you in Christ Jesus." Does that really say "in *all* circumstances"? Does "all" mean the good *and* the bad? Did Paul really mean to give thanks in the difficult times? Yes! Paul knew what it meant to give thanks and rejoice in the good *and* the bad. Paul was beaten, abused, falsely accused, and thrown in prison, amongst other horrible things, and instead of moaning and groaning, he is depicted as singing praise and thanksgiving to God. Paul was thankful in *all* circumstances. He wrote the books of Ephesians, Philippians, Colossians, 2 Timothy, and Philemon from inside the walls of a prison cell.

David is another awesome example of a man who gave thanks no matter what his circumstances looked like. In the

> *"Give thanks in all circumstances; for this is God's will for you in Christ Jesus."*

book of Psalms, we are privileged to see his transparency as he poured out his heart to God during times of extreme pain and suffering. Yet, in the same book we are exposed to his overwhelming heart of gratitude to God despite his troubles.

Jesus gave us the ultimate example of giving thanks in all things as He broke bread with His friends in the upper room, knowing that His agonizing death was just hours away.

God adores a heart of gratitude! If we truly believe Romans 8:28 which states, "And we know that in all things God works for the good of those who love Him, who have been called according to His purpose," then we can thank God even in the worst of circumstances. We can trust He is working it all out for our good. When we look at the main characters in the Bible, they are often found giving thanks to God even when everything around them appears to be in turmoil. They would not allow their faith to be shaken by their situation, hardships, troubles, or fears. They continued to operate with hearts of thankfulness, trusting that God was working behind the scenes for their benefit and for the greater good.

With tears of joy, I remember the day I trotted up my garage stairs with ease, carrying three bags of groceries. I opened the door to my kitchen and yelled, "Thank You God! I love my life!" I plopped the groceries on the floor and fell to my knees weeping as I remembered the day, only one year earlier, that I had dragged myself up those very same stairs in pain and weakness, fell to the floor sobbing and yelled out, "I hate my life!" I had been ill with numerous auto-immune disorders. I had become so handicapped that even the simple task of grocery shopping became one of my worst nightmares. One year later, I was rejoicing at all the healing that had taken place in my life. I am here to encourage you to start thanking God for what He *is* doing, and to stop complaining and grumbling about what you think He is *not* doing. God is always up to something, and it is always for our benefit, for the greater good of the world. Remember that most of us only see with physical eyes, but God and His angels are moving in the spiritual realm on our behalf. As I look back over all the years of sickness, all the times of hardship, and all the times I was offended or hurt by others, I rejoice knowing that God was making me mature and complete, lacking nothing (James 1:2–4, HCSB).

Smith Wigglesworth puts it like this:

> Some people think they are tried more than other people. Trials are used to purify you; it is the fiery furnace of affliction that God uses to get you in the place where he can use you. The person who has no trials and no difficulties is the person whom God does not dare allow Satan to touch because this person could not stand temptation. But Jesus will not allow any man to be tempted more than he is able to bear... If you knew the value of trials, you would praise God for them more than for anything.[2]

I have started a new practice. When I receive bad news, or when something goes wrong in my life, my region, or my nation, I stop and give thanks. This may sound ludicrous to you, but God delights in a heart of thankfulness, and I tell you it makes the enemy roar! It sabotages every scheme the devil has planned for evil. The other day I found myself stuck in 100-degree weather in horrible traffic on an eight-lane California freeway. I started singing at the top of my lungs, "Thank You, God, for this traffic! Thank You for this special time with You! Thank You that You are working all things together for my good! Thank You for my vehicle that is comfortable and air conditioned!" I then went on to pray for each person in every car around me. It changed my whole attitude from, *This is horrible; I'm going to be late,* to moving mountains in the spiritual realm. I began to thank God for allowing me to impact the destiny of each person in every car around me as I prayed for them. I know that someday I am going to get to heaven and one or more of those people will run up to me and thank me for interceding for them! I also know without a doubt that angels were watching over me. You never know what kind of accident or incident I may have been spared from by being detained in traffic. God knows, and I trust Him with my life.

I had two choices that day. I could have sat in my car stressed out, thinking over and over about how late I was going to be, allowing my blood pressure to rise, and imagining the worst; or I could thank the Lord knowing and trusting that He was taking care of things for me. "Many are the plans in a person's heart, but it is the LORD's purpose that prevails" (Proverbs 19:21). The Lord's purposes are significantly better than any dreams or plans I can concoct on my own. I choose to surrender, knowing that if I miss my flight, receive a deadly diagnosis from a doctor, or hear bad news of earthquakes, war, famine, hurricanes, or tornados, I can trust that the Lord is orchestrating His divine purposes on the earth for my benefit and for His glory.

## The Testing

As I've been reflecting on this chapter, I have been tested on this very issue. It is currently the month of January and I have been laid up in bed now for four weeks. While spreading joy, delivering Christmas goodies to our neighbors one cold December evening, I was majorly sideswiped. It happened one week before Christmas when I still had a list a mile long to complete. Delivering Christmas gift baskets was one task I had been looking forward to. It has always been such fun to surprise people with unexpected blessings. We had been out singing carols and rejoicing as we walked from one neighbor's house to the next. Suddenly, in the dark of the night, my foot stepped onto uneven ground, my ankle twisted and rolled, my knee snapped out sideways from my body, I heard a loud crack, and I was thrown to the ground in severe pain. I cried out as I laid on the hard pavement. My family tried to leverage me off of the road, but I was in shock and unable to move. My husband ran back to get the car, lifted me in, and quickly transported me home.

As I sat on the couch by the fireplace, leg elevated with ice, waiting for the pain reliever to kick in, I cried and cried. The pain was excruciating and my mind immediately began going to a negative place. I had just had surgery on that same knee only a few months earlier. It was Christmas and we had numerous plans including a pre-holiday getaway to the ocean for a couple of nights to celebrate my sister-in-law's birthday. I still had to clean and prepare the house since guests would be arriving shortly after the trip. I had last minute shopping to do, groceries to buy and meal prep to attend to. Laundry and packing needed to be done, as well as gift wrapping. All of my children would be coming home to celebrate our Savior's birth, and I had been planning and dreaming of the wonderful family time we would have together.

An x-ray determined a fractured ankle that would require surgery, plates, screws, a hook, and a minimum three-month recovery flat on my back. The next morning as I laid in bed in terrible pain, the enemy rushed in and immediately began to take me to a dark place. He reminded me loud and clear that all my plans were nothing now, that everything was ruined. The one week I had left to prepare for the perfect Christmas would now be filled with doctor appointments, lab tests, surgery, and pain. I became angry.

I cried out to God, whining about all of my ruined plans. He was quick to remind me of the truths I had been writing, preaching, and speaking to others about over the past few years. I heard Him say, "Daughter, do you really believe the things you write and speak about Me?" "Of course I do!" I retorted. "Then walk it out in

---
*Walk it out in faith.*
---

faith." He replied. It has been a month now and I am literally walking it out. I began to change my whines and complaints to thanksgiving. "Thank You God that I get to spend more time with You. Thank You that I get to spend uninterrupted time working on this book while recovering with my leg elevated. Thank You for my warm house and comfortable bed where I can rest in Your peace. Thank You that You are my healer. Thank You that I get to bless and encourage others through emails, texts, phone calls, and Facebook messages. Thank You that You are working on my attitude. Thank You for molding me and shaping me through this trial."

After much prayer, I decided against having the surgery and instead am choosing to decree healing Scriptures over my bones, to worship God, to pray in tongues, and to give thanks through all of it. I am being encouraged by the Lord every day and my faith is rising!

Update: Today, January 24th, I returned to the doctor for a follow-up appointment and am ecstatic to testify that the x-rays show that my bones have healed in perfect alignment and I can begin weight-bearing exercises. All glory to Jehovah Rapha, my healer!!! To say I am thankful is an understatement!

Let's pray:

Lord, teach us to be thankful. Teach Your children to rejoice and give thanks in *all* things, even when the world seems to be spinning out of control. May we have thankful hearts amidst the tears. Make us well up with gratitude as we recognize that You truly are working all things for the best interest of Your Ekklesia. We love You and thank You for taking on our iniquities, infirmities, anxieties, and fears. Thank You that You took the beating for us and died a horrific death on the cross, so we could truly live in peace and joy. We love You and are full of unending gratitude. Help us to see with Your eyes from heaven's perspective. May we begin to trust You in the midst of chaos. Fill us with Your peace. We choose to have thankful hearts. We choose Your joy and Your peace. Allow us to be carriers of that joy and peace everywhere we go and in every season. In Jesus' name we pray. Amen.

CHAPTER 7

## *Forgive*

*And when you stand praying, if you hold
anything against anyone,
forgive them, so that your Father in heaven
may forgive you your sins.*

*Mark 11:25*

Unfortunately, betrayal is not an uncommon part of life in the Ekklesia. Most of us have been betrayed by one whom we love at some point in our lives. This can be one of the most painful experiences a person has to live through. We expect people to treat us poorly at times, but when we are betrayed by someone we deeply love and care for—a family member, a brother or sister in the Lord, a church, or an organization that we serve with and trust—it can feel unbearable. Not too long ago I went through an extremely difficult season.

I experienced the most painful betrayal of my entire adulthood. This is an excerpt from my journal that I wrote four months into the experience:

> The betrayal of a family member, close friend, or a loved one is one of the most painful experiences an individual should ever have to endure in life. Your heart is broken. Your trust is severed. It feels like all life has been sucked out of you, and your bones have been crushed beyond repair. It feels as if your heart is being ripped out of you from the inside out. Depression invades the soul and your mind becomes cloudy. You are unable to focus or see things from a clear perspective. It can take weeks, months, even years to feel healing or peace from the pain. It is as if every last breath is an intense labor trying to escape from your chest. The days are long, cold, sterile… but the nights are even longer, as you play over and over in your mind the harsh words of death that were spoken to you, over you, at you, about you. They haunt you into the wee hours of the morning. You long for sleep. You cry out to God. You feel nothing but pain. Peace has left. Joy has been stolen. The pain is unbearable. Despair invades. Your thinking becomes irrational. Will life ever be okay again?
>
> Betrayal can feel worse than a death. Because when someone you love dies, they are gone from the earth. When you are betrayed, however, the person is still there. They are still a part of your world. You may still have to see them, hear them, hear about them, hear from them. The wound to the heart can be devastating. Heart wounds are often worse than a bruise, beating, or cut to the body; for physical wounds to the body heal quickly. You can watch the changes to the color in your skin, the new cells replacing the damaged cells. The bleeding turns to

a scab. The scab falls off. The scar forms. Then over time, the scar becomes less noticeable. A wound to the heart, however, takes its toll down to the very depths of your soul. It damages your thoughts, which in turn depletes your energy, your stamina, and everything that makes you function in a healthy manner. Only God can heal a heart wound.

By the grace of God, I made it through that season and came out even stronger than I was, but I had to make a choice. The Lord required something of me. The choice was to forgive. I had been wronged, betrayed, and severely wounded by those whom I deeply loved. It took months of daily choosing to forgive, bless, and release those who had hurt me. I prayed for them each day. I spoke forgiveness out loud. I blessed them. I asked the Lord to let me see them through His eyes and to bless everything they put their hands to. Through the months of tears, loneliness, and sadness, the Lord did surgery on my heart and gave me His heart for my betrayers. He also gave me a heart of repentance that I wouldn't trade for all the pain I endured. I learned what it really meant to forgive seventy times seven (Matthew 18:22), even when lies and gossip continued to circulate, even when there seemed to be no end to the slander, even when I had to face my persecutors regularly.

Psalm 4:1–3 became near and dear to my heart. I would cry out to God in the dark hours of the night with David's words:

> Answer me when I call,
> God, who vindicates me.
> You freed me from affliction;
> be gracious to me and hear my prayer.
>
> How long, exalted men, will my honor be insulted?
> How long will you love what is worthless
> and pursue a lie? *Selah*

Know that the LORD has set apart
the faithful for Himself;
the LORD will hear when I call to Him. (HCSB)

David understood betrayal and faced it on more than one occasion. In Psalm 55:12–14, he wrote these verses that resonated with my heart and the anguish I was feeling:

It wasn't an enemy who taunted me.
If it was my enemy, filled with pride and hatred,
then I could have endured it. I would have just run away.
But it was you, my intimate friend—one like a brother to me.
It was you, my advisor, the companion I walked with
and worked with!
We once had sweet fellowship with each other.
We worshiped in unity as one,
celebrating together with God's people. (TPT)

The reason betrayal is so painful is because it comes at you like a blow from one whom you never expected or believed would ever hurt you. David experienced the pain of betrayal by a loved one, but he never got ahead of God, and he never gave in to the temptation to get even. David had several opportunities to get revenge, but he was a man after God's own heart and never took matters into his own hands. As he allowed God to move and have His way, God always protected David and brought him out even stronger after each betrayal he faced. David had a heart that knew how to forgive because he trusted God knew what He was doing, no matter how difficult or painful the road became.

## The Key

Forgiveness is a key to every crisis. Holding onto unforgiveness only breeds resentment and bitterness. It doesn't do a thing to the person we are refusing to forgive. It only keeps us hostage in a prison of our own mind, playing and re-playing things over and over again. Forgiveness unlocks healing. Forgiveness allows us to live out the future in freedom, knowing that no matter what our circumstances look like, we have opened the door to moving forward into a future that is full and bright. "For if you forgive other people when they sin against you, your heavenly Father will also forgive you. But if you do not forgive others their sins, your Father will not forgive your sins" (Matthew 6:14–15). Ouch!

Recently I read this on a sign in an office I was visiting:

The first to apologize is the bravest.
The first to forgive is the strongest.
The first to forget is the happiest.
Author Unknown

I don't know whom to give credit to for these words, but they are brilliant. There is such truth in that little saying. God has been moving my heart to apologize and ask for forgiveness even when I think I am right. It always takes two to mess things up. We can never place full blame on the other person. We can't take responsibility for them, but we surely can, and must, take responsibility for our part in the conflict.

Forgiveness is a difficult thing. It is a most humbling experience to ask somebody who has wronged you to forgive you, but that is exactly what Christ calls us to do. It takes two or more parties to have conflict. We must own up to our part, repent, and leave the rest to God. He is our defender and our vindicator.

Several months back I felt led to apologize to someone who, in my mind, was totally to blame. I didn't want to repent, but the Lord's conviction was so strong that I knew I had to be obedient. I went to the person and asked for her forgiveness. She put her hand up in my face, refused the apology, and spurted out some ugly words. I wanted to verbally fight back, but instead, I asked her forgiveness one last time before turning to walk away. She was rude and downright cruel to me. Instead of feeling rejection and anger, a flood of peace came over me because I knew I had been faithful, even though it was not well received. I had been obedient to God and thus had been set free. I walked away with a clean conscience and a pure heart. I blessed the person and released her to God.

Matthew 18:7 reports that offenses *will* come. We can be sure of that. Satan uses the weakness and ignorance in people to offend. Ignorance allows people to speak out of a well-meaning heart or what they consider a "good idea," but that doesn't mean it's a God idea. Words spoken carelessly can become a plot of the devil to divert the plan of God in your life. Harboring bitterness and unforgiveness can derail a believer from their destiny, especially when it comes from someone in the church. It boils down to human understanding versus supernatural understanding. The truth is, there is absolutely no room for offense. Your faith may be tested, but you must get over offenses quickly or you will get derailed. Every offense brings an occasion to fall. Each offense can become a stumbling block if you allow it to. An offense can be anything that gets between you and God. You must not give the offender the power to steal your destiny.

*Harboring bitterness and unforgiveness can derail a believer from their destiny.*

## Don't Get Robbed of the Anointing

I grew up learning to hold on to offenses. Negative things were spoken and repeated and stewed over. I realized I had held on to offenses my entire life. My relatives had offended me. My friends had offended me. My classmates had offended me. My coworkers had offended me. Even my brothers and sisters in the Lord had offended me. That is a part of life! What matters is what we do with the offense. It is pertinent that we learn to let go and release the offender. I had to learn to forgive and move on. I was only hurting myself by holding onto unforgiveness. I had become captive and tripped up by the offenses I had been holding on to. I had to repent and let go of the offenses, as well as the people who had offended me. I pictured myself placing the cross between myself and my offenders. Christ died for them and for me.

I came to the realization that I was robbing myself of God's anointing and of walking into the healing promised to me by Jesus' death and resurrection, because of the unforgiveness I was holding in my heart. My soul had become sick and polluted by bitterness and unforgiveness. As soon as I began to get my heart healed up, my body began to heal. It was a process. I asked the Lord to bring to my mind each person from my past toward whom I was holding unforgiveness. Then one by one I forgave them, pictured the cross of Jesus between us, pleaded the blood of Jesus over the offense, blessed them, and released them. God had been so gracious to forgive me over and over again. What right did I have to hold others to a different standard? My sick heart was making for a sick body.

*We must not allow offense to overtake us and rob us of our divine destiny.*

We are sons and daughters of the Living God. We have sonship benefits. If God has given us the divine nature and very essence of Himself, then why do we fall short of living out all of these promises? If we are truly partakers of all that is available through the risen Christ, then we have to quit entertaining offense in our minds. Offense can easily take root in a person's heart, along with the many emotions that come with it. We must not allow offense to overtake us and rob us of our divine destiny.

## Walk in Peace

Five years ago, I received a devastating phone call from a family member that turned my world upside-down. I remember going through many different stages when I received the phone call. First I blamed myself. Then I began to blame everybody else I could think of. It got pretty crazy in my head, and the Lord called me on it. When I finally repented, took my eyes off of everyone else, and began working on myself, I was able to think more clearly. I was set free for God to begin healing my own broken heart. Psalm 119:165 has become ever dear to me as I face future tumultuous situations. I insert my name when decreeing out loud, "Abundant peace belongs to Debbie, who loves Your instruction. Nothing makes me stumble" (paraphrased). As I daily decree this word over my life, I see myself getting stronger, not so easily frazzled and tossed by the winds and offenses of life.

People will still wound us, but once we align our hearts and minds with God's truth, the wounds won't have the sting. As we pick up our shield of faith (Ephesians 6:16), the arrows and daggers the enemy throws our way will bounce right off of us.

Pray for God to help you release those you may be blaming for the situation you are currently facing. I have a friend who blames her husband for their marriage struggles. I have another friend who blames her ex-husband for the rebellion of their children. Another friend blames her daughter's boyfriend for providing her daughter with drugs. Many in our nation blame our president for the way things are going. Personally, I often found myself blaming others when things were not going well in my life. As I repented and asked the Lord for His heart, everything changed. I began to see those who I viewed as "the enemy" as God sees them, and I began to love them as He loves them. Often, those who wound us are deeply wounded and broken people themselves. You've probably heard the statement, "Hurting people hurt people." Those who offend us are not the enemy. We know who the enemy is. He is the one who comes to steal, kill, and destroy (John 10:10).

If you find yourself stuck in a cycle of bitterness, anger, resentment, jealousy, or grief, command your spirit to arise in joy and peace. Don't allow your emotions to control you. Tell yourself how to feel! Speak to your spirit and command it to align with the truth of God in your heart, "for the joy of the LORD is your strength" (Nehemiah 8:10).

Remember also to always walk in grace towards one another. That grumpy cashier ringing up your groceries and throwing them into your bag may be going through a bitter divorce. That rude receptionist checking you in at the doctor's office may have recently lost her baby. The guy cutting you off in traffic on your way to work may have just been diagnosed with a serious illness. We never really know what is going on in the hearts and minds of others. I am finding it is always best to give them the benefit of the doubt. The *old* me would have griped and complained or even lashed back at them. The *new* me gives them a compliment or offers to pray for them. You never know the impact that one kind word will have on someone going through a bad season.

I have a friend who loves to share the story of the day she was super sad and barely made it to work. Having been sick with cancer, she had undergone treatments, lost all her hair, and was feeling lousy. She pulled herself together and made it to work, but was feeling horrible about how her hair had grown back in. She felt she was having a really bad hair day and was feeling pretty miserable about herself. She passed by a gentleman in the bank where she worked. He paused, looked her in the eyes and said, "Your hair is absolutely beautiful!" This man had no idea the impact his words had on my friend in that moment. His simple comment altered her entire mood. That is the heart of God. He knew my friend intimately, knew how terrible she was feeling about her hair, and sent an angel of love to bless her regarding the very issue she was struggling with. In my friend's words, "His statement shifted my whole day."

Lord, help us to be atmosphere-shifters and destiny-changers. Remind us that "our struggle is not against flesh and blood, but against the rulers, against the authorities, against the powers of this dark world and against the spiritual forces of evil in the heavenly realms" (Ephesians 6:12). Help us, Lord, to forgive our betrayers, and anyone we are holding hostage in our minds. We repent for not having Your heart and for walking outside of Your perfect peace. Forgive us, Lord, and give us Your mind over our difficulties. Give us Your eyes to see others how You see them. Give us Your love for those who have offended us. We decree that "No weapon that is formed against Your Ekklesia shall prosper; and every tongue that shall rise against us in judgment we shall condemn. This is the heritage of the servants of the LORD, and their righteousness is of Me, says the LORD" (Isaiah 54:17, AKJV paraphrased). We bless those who have persecuted us and we release them. They are Yours. Have Your way. Bring Your church back to the plans You have for us. Thank You for the power that is released in our lives when we choose to forgive. In Jesus' name we pray. Amen.

CHAPTER 8

# The Blood of Jesus

*How much more, then, will the blood of Christ,
who through the eternal Spirit offered
Himself unblemished to God,
cleanse our consciences from acts that lead to death,
so that we may serve the living God!*

Hebrews 9:14

My dear friend, Sheri, was staying at a cabin up in the mountains for a wonderful week of vacation with extended family members. The first day there, she was out on a hike, stepped off the narrow road to allow a truck pulling a boat to pass by, twisted her ankle, and fell to the ground. She arose in terrible pain and managed to hobble back to the cabin. Through the course of the next several hours her foot swelled up and the pain became unbearable, leading to a trip to the nearest emergency room. Upon doctor observation and an x-ray, it was determined that she had fractured her foot. As the doctor left the room after giving the report, Sheri looked at her husband and said, "Whose report are we going to believe?" They agreed in that moment to not receive the doctor's report, and instead to embrace and believe the report of the Lord. Jesus said He came to deliver, heal, and set us free (Luke 4:18).

Sheri left the hospital with pain meds in hand, limping back to the cabin on a pair of crutches. Throughout the week she stayed in the cabin with her foot elevated, icing it as much as possible. Though the week was not spent enjoying the great outdoors with her family, she had an intimate week indoors with her healer Jesus Christ. As everyone else was out hiking, boating, swimming, and having fun, Sheri laid back on an ottoman pleading the blood of Jesus Christ over her foot. She determined in her heart that God's Word was true, would have the final say in her life, and that at the end of the week, she would walk out of that cabin on two feet without crutches. And that is exactly what she did! To this day her foot is healthy and whole. She walks and runs on it with ease. She has full mobility and no pain. To God be the glory!

## Transformative Power

I don't think I will ever comprehend, this side of heaven, the power in the blood of Jesus and what He accomplished on the cross. The blood of Jesus covers *all*. He willingly shed His blood to cover all of the sins, shortcomings, failings, sickness, evil, and wickedness of the earth. That is some kind of unfathomable, incomprehensible love. Everything Christ did for you at the cross completes you and makes you whole, new, pure, clean, spotless, unafraid, and unashamed. It's who you are! It's who He made you to be! Only God can take a messed-up, chaotic, out of control life, and completely transform it by

His blood. That is exactly what He has done for me, for you, for our spouses, for our children, and for the Ekklesia! His blood offers deliverance, restoration, salvation, transformation, healing, hope, destiny, and so much more.

I once heard Bill Johnson, Senior Pastor at Bethel Church in Redding, California, speak about the power of the blood of Jesus.[1] He was teaching from the Old Testament and pointed out that when the Israelites sinned, they had to take a pure, spotless animal and sacrifice it. There had to be innocent blood shed to atone for the sin. The incredible thing I had not taken note of before is that only *one* animal had to be killed and sacrificed *per family*. They did not have to slaughter one lamb for dad, another for mom, and more for each child. They were only required to shed the blood of *one animal per household*. This was revelation to me! Pastor Bill went on to explain that as a parent, I have the authority to plead the blood of Jesus over my children. My son or daughter may have sinned, but as their mom, I can step in and plead the shed blood of Jesus Christ, His finished work on the cross, over my children.

When I heard this, I couldn't wait for my husband to come home. He walked in the door and I practically pounced him with the news. I had communion all ready. The poor guy came in, hungry for dinner after a long day at work, and the table was set with those small communion cups filled with grape juice, and a tiny little cracker on each plate. His smile turned to a downward frown—but only for a second. As I began explaining to him what I had learned, his excitement began to match mine and we started praying for everything that was out of alignment with the will of God for our family. That night was the start of something we practice many evenings per week together. We regularly plead the blood of Jesus over our marriage, our children, our finances, our property, our home, our vehicles, our jobs, our ministries, and everything we lay our hands to. We have seen God's faithfulness time and time again when the enemy rises up and attempts to attack and take us out. The blood of Jesus is timeless and already did what He meant for it to do. His blood covers all.

This is a heavenly strategy that the devil cannot stand up against. When Jesus conquered sin and death on the cross, the game was changed forever. All we have to do is acknowledge what He did, thank Him for it, and receive this free gift. There are no tricks, gimmicks, or false expectations. Parents always like to tell their kids that there is no free lunch in life, meaning nothing is free, that everything comes with a price. However, I am here to proclaim that there *is* something free, so free that it is truly incomprehensible: the free gift of salvation and eternal life! And the beauty of it all is that as a parent, I have the authority to decree it and call it forth for my family and my entire household! Woo-hoo! Can you feel my excitement? Jesus already paid the price. Thank you, Lord! "In Him we have redemption through His blood, the forgiveness of our trespasses, according to the riches of His grace" (Ephesians 1:7, ESV).

If you are chronically ill, I encourage you to begin taking communion daily as you would take daily medication. Decree Isaiah 53:5 over yourself. Watch the blood of Jesus restore your health.

I have fond memories of being a young mom and singing the song "Nothing but the Blood of Jesus"[2] with my youngest daughter as I tucked her in at night. At the time, they were just beautiful words with a fun tune that I loved hearing my baby girl sing. As I have grown closer to the Lord, I am in awe of the sacrifice He made for me and for you. Back then I did not understand, and my mind could not fully comprehend, the immensity of the blood of Jesus. To this day it is hard to imagine that a perfect, loving Father would send His *only* beloved Son down to earth to pay the penalty for

> *Pleading the blood of Jesus is by far the most important and significant strategy of them all.*

my humanness, my carnality, and my wicked heart. I am the mother of three children, and I cannot think of a single person I would sacrifice one of my beloved babies for. Yet God, because of His immense love for me, for you, and for the whole human race, sent His Son out of heaven to live on earth. Jesus suffered intense persecution, ridicule, torment, abuse, evil, and torture of every kind, ultimately ending in the most horrific death known to mankind. He did this for me, for you, and for anyone who will receive Him and acknowledge Him as Lord. What a mind-blowing concept! Too big for this human mind to conceive!

Do you realize that,

Jesus became human to fully identify with us. He did this so that He could experience death and annihilate the effects of the intimidating accuser who holds against us the power of death. By embracing death, Jesus sets free those who live their entire lives in bondage to the tormenting dread of death. (Hebrews 2:14–15, TPT)

If there is any unconfessed sin in your life, take care of it right now. Don't wait! Allow the Holy Spirit to convict you immediately any time you stray from the heart of God. This will allow you to keep hearing the voice of the Lord clearly. It will keep your heart tender and in line with God's plans and purposes for you. Heed His discipline. Free yourself through the blood of Jesus.

Hebrews 12:10–12 in The Passion Translation reads:

God corrects us throughout our lives for our own good, giving us an invitation to share His holiness. Now all discipline seems to be more pain than pleasure at the time, yet later it will produce a transformation of character, bringing a harvest of righteousness and peace to those who yield to it. So be made strong even in your weakness by lifting up your tired hands *in prayer and worship*. And strengthen your weak knees, for as you keep walking forward on God's paths all your stumbling ways will be divinely healed!

**Pleading the blood of Jesus is by far the most important and significant strategy of them all. His blood promises to bring transformation to every broken place in your life.**

Pray with me:

Lord, thank You that as a member of Your Ekklesia, I have the power and authority to plead the blood of Jesus over every crisis, and over every sin in my life and in the world around me. I call forth the destiny that You have for me, my family, my region, and my nation. Bring my life back into alignment with Your plans and purposes to fulfill every page of my destiny that was written before I was even conceived! Lord, I will not relent until You fulfill every promise. You are God. You never fail, and You are ever faithful. Thank You that I can hold fast to the vision You have for my life. Remind me that when I keep my eyes on Your truth and Your vision, nothing can get me down or defeat me. I choose today to stand on Your promises and to call them forth. I plead the blood of Jesus over every place in my life, my household, my state, and my nation that is out of alignment. Thank You, Lord, for shedding Your blood and for dying for Your Ekklesia. In Jesus' name, I keep my eyes on You. Amen.

## CHAPTER 9

# Generational Sin and Curses

*But from everlasting to everlasting
the LORD's love is with those who fear Him,
and His righteousness with their children's children —*

Psalm 103:17

I once heard a friend say, "My father died from a heart attack at a young age, my grandfather died of a heart attack at a young age, and my great-grandfather died of a heart attack at a young age. I probably will too!" I cringed when I heard the words he confessed out of

> ... what we speak, we become.

his mouth. I had learned the biblical lesson that the power of life and death is in the tongue (Proverbs 18:21). Looking back through history, I see a common thread that what we speak, we become. What we say most often happens to us. This is a biblical principal. We usually attract what we speak. God spoke the world into being, and it was so. Our words hold power. We create our world by what we speak.

Personally, I used to yell at my kids when I was having a migraine or was experiencing pain. They were just being normal, energetic children. Yet my tolerance level was being affected by my physical condition, so I would yell out, "You kids are driving me crazy!" What eventually happened? I was slowly going crazy. Many a day I felt as if I was losing it mentally. As the years progressed, I knew I was going off the deep end, but I didn't know how to stop the downward spiral.

By the grace of God, I was made aware of this concept before my life had plunged completely out of control. Just five years ago I could not memorize anything, and I really felt as if I was losing my mind. I blamed my illnesses for my mental decline. As I began learning the power that my words carry and the even greater power of God's words, I determined I would memorize one Bible verse if nothing else. I began saying out loud every day, "For God has not given me the spirit of fear; but of power, and of love, and of a sound mind" (2 Timothy 1:7, AKJV, paraphrased). So what happened? As I began reciting this verse, I was soon able to memorize it. I then began to pray it over other people. God walked me into a sound mind as I decreed His Word over my life. I am now able to memorize Scripture and am walking out of all fear. I give all glory to God!

I know another family who has a saying, "All of the women in our family go crazy as they get older." I have heard numerous women in this family repeat those words, and unfortunately, I have seen many of the older women get diagnosed with dementia or Alzheimer's disease. My response is, let it stop with you! Don't speak it out and partner with it. The enemy loves nothing more than for us to verbally agree with his attack on our family bloodline. It gives him full permission to swoop in and bring it to pass.

## Break the Curse

Is there such a thing as generational sin or a generational curse? What does that even mean? Can I really be cursed because of something my ancestors did hundreds of years ago? Absolutely! Exodus 20:4–6 speaks of visiting the iniquity of the fathers on the children to the third and fourth generations:

> Do not make an idol for yourself, whether in the shape of anything in the heavens above or on the earth below or in the waters under the earth. You must not bow down to them or worship them; for I, the LORD your God, am a jealous God, punishing the children for the fathers' sin, to the third and fourth generations of those who hate Me, but showing faithful love to a thousand generations of those who love Me and keep my commands. (HCSB)

Graeme Walsh, Associate Director of the Santa Maria Valley Healing Rooms and Apostolic Center, writes in his workbook "Generational Sin and Curses": "Curses can be consequences or results of sin (also known as iniquity) which are activated when we break God's Word or laws. If those sins are not repented of, there is a consequence. These sins can affect subsequent generations of our family."[1] Wow! As this biblical truth was revealed to me, I had to go back and ask the Lord to bring to light the sins of my ancestors. I was determined that the curse would stop with me, with my generation. When I looked back at the generational sins within my family bloodline, I could see patterns of alcoholism, sexual sin, suicide, depression, anxiety, gossip, pride, and involvement with Freemasonry. I was able to visualize some of the effects of these sins trickling down through the generations. I began to confess the sins of my ancestors to the Lord and asked Him to let it stop with me.

The good news is that God is a God of grace and mercy. Did you catch Exodus 20:6 above? He shows "faithful love to a thousand generations of those who love Me and keep My commands." Thank You, Lord! Christ died for my sins and for my family's sins. As a daughter of the King, I have authority to stand before my heavenly Father in the courtroom of heaven and plead innocent because of what Jesus did for me! Jesus took on *all* of my sins and *all* of my ancestors' sins when He was nailed to the cross at Calvary: "'He Himself bore our sins' in His body on the cross, so that we might die to sins and live for righteousness; 'by His wounds you have been healed'" (1 Peter 2:24). If that is truly the case, then we can stand before a holy God and all He sees is Jesus. Jesus is the ultimate sacrifice who stands between us and the Father and vouches for our innocence, our purity, and our righteousness. The Father only sees the Son in His Ekklesia.

There are numerous ways generational curses can affect our bloodline. Some curses we might not even be aware of. I find great solace in the fact that I can confess any unknown sins to my Lord on behalf of my ancestors and break their power. God is the same God yesterday, today, and forever (Hebrews 13:8). This means there are no time constraints with Him. He can go into my past and the past of my ancestors and bring the sin to the present so I can repent in their place. I can confess the sins of my fathers and receive ultimate forgiveness, freedom, and blessing for my children and my children's children to the thousandth generation. What a concept!

Did you hear that? We can become free from the curse. It's a free gift available to anyone who wants it. Let sin and generational curses end with you. You have the authority to stop them in their tracks and remove the power of the enemy from your family bloodline. Do you notice a pattern of illness or sin in your family? Maybe it's cancer, diabetes, obesity, alcoholism, drug addiction, or homosexuality? Do you see something that has been carried down through the generations? Maybe it's depression, anxiety, addiction to pornography, gluttony, poverty, or getting pregnant out of wedlock. Whatever it is, Jesus holds the key to set you and your family free.

Find a quiet spot. Get on your knees and ask the Lord to forgive the sins of your ancestors. Ask the Lord to forgive and break off every word curse you have knowingly or unknowingly confessed over yourself or your family. As a child of God, you have the privilege of pleading the blood of Jesus over every sin you and your ancestors have committed. It's time to take back everything the enemy has stolen from your family bloodline. Scripture encourages us: "'No weapon that is formed against you or your family will prosper; and every tongue that accuses you in judgment you will condemn. This is the heritage of the servants of the LORD, and their vindication is from Me,' declares the LORD" (Isaiah 54:17, paraphrased). Decree it out loud!

Walsh's book highlights two family bloodlines and the consequences of their actions:

> Around the beginning of the 20$^{th}$ century, a Mr. E.E. Winship published studies of two well-known American families of the 19$^{th}$ century. His findings have been featured in many publications since that date and are well worth passing on.
>
> Max Jukes was an atheist who married a godless woman. Some 560 descendants were traced. Of these:
>
> - 310 died as paupers.
> - 150 became criminals, 7 of them murderers.
> - 100 were known to be drunkards.

- More than half the women were prostitutes.
- In all, the descendants of Max Jukes cost the U.S. Government over $1,250,000 19th-century dollars.

Jonathan Edwards was a contemporary of Max Jukes. He was a committed Christian who married a godly young lady. Some 1,394 descendants were traced. Of these:

- 295 graduated from college, from whom 13 became college presidents, and 65 became professors.
- 3 were elected as United States senators, 3 as state governors, and others sent as ministers to foreign countries.
- 30 were judges.
- 100 were lawyers, one the dean of an outstanding law school.
- 56 practiced as physicians, one was the dean of a medical school.
- 75 became officers in the Army and Navy.
- 100 became well known missionaries, preachers, and prominent authors.
- 80 held some sort of public office, of whom 3 were mayors of large cities.
- One was the controller of the U.S. Treasury, another a Vice-President of the United States.
- Not one of the descendants of the Edwards family was a liability to the government.[2]

Those are some amazing statistics. What kind of legacy do you want to leave? One that is cursed and takes from society? Or one that is a blessing to society? For more information, or to go deeper with this topic, refer to the notes section in the back of this book for some suggested reading.[3]

Let's pray:

Lord, I come before You and acknowledge that You are my Lord and Savior. I thank You for dying on the cross for my sins and for the sins of my ancestors. I repent for and renounce the sins and curses of my family bloodline. Thank You that You exchanged the curses for blessings when You died on the cross.

I decree and declare freedom for my children and my children's children for generations to come. I break off every curse, both known and unknown, and I decree that my descendants will walk in the blessings of the Lord to the thousandth generation per Your Word. In the name of Jesus Christ my Lord. Amen.

CHAPTER 10

# Anointing Oil & Prayer Cloths

*Is anyone among you sick?
Let them call the elders of the church to pray over them
and anoint them with oil in the name of the Lord.*

James 5:14

I attended a conference of a traveling, prophetic, healing evangelist several years ago. During the conference, people were going up to the front of the room and throwing their jackets, scarves, gloves, and other articles of clothing onto the stage. The stage became so full of garments that the evangelist had to keep pushing them over with his feet so he could maneuver around the stage. I thought to myself, *This is the strangest thing ever!* I asked my friend what it was all about. She told me that the evangelist and his team would pray over the clothing. Then the individuals would take their items home and place them on their sick relatives or friends and believe for their healing.

The next morning, I opened my Bible and began to search the Scriptures. I was amazed at what I found. In Acts 19:11–12 it is recorded that "God was performing extraordinary miracles by Paul's hands, so that even facecloths or aprons that had touched his skin were brought to the sick, and the diseases left them, and the evil spirits came out of them" (CSB). I began pondering the significance of this. If I am a disciple of Jesus and I am supposed to be doing greater things than even He did when He was on earth (John 14:12), then this was another strategy from heaven I should be implementing. The Lord brought to mind the woman mentioned in Matthew 9:20–22 who had been bleeding for twelve long years. She pressed through the huge crowds and managed to touch the hem of Jesus' cloak, believing this simple contact would heal her. Jesus responded telling her, "Your faith has made you well." It's not the cloth or garment that does the healing. It is the Lord Jesus Christ through our simple act of faith.

I decided to begin putting this strategy into practice. I started to anoint handkerchiefs and pieces of fabric with oil and began to pray over them. Whenever my adult children come home for a visit, I place one of these in their pillowcase. (Don't tell them about my secret weapon!) I ask the Lord to heal and to bring into alignment any place in their lives that is not in His perfect will. I also pray that He will give them dreams and visions from heaven while they sleep on that pillow at night. I have been amazed at the things that have been brought to light over the years and the revelation received from the Lord.

## *Testimony Time*

A few years ago a couple of friends and I were asked to minister to a group of women in a town two hours away. We had been anointing and praying over some cloths for a conference we were going to host, so we decided to take some with us. We distributed a cloth to each person as a gift and explained what they were for. About a month later we received a call from the leader of this group. She recounted a testimony about one of their ladies who had been struggling with severe abdominal pain. They remembered the prayer cloths and laid one over her stomach. She was instantly healed! This is not magic or hocus-pocus. It's not a system, but a point of contact. This is a biblical concept that we have the power and authority to implement. If you are unable to physically go and pray for someone, anoint a handkerchief or piece of cloth, pray over it, and send it by mail. If your marriage is struggling, anoint, pray over, and place a handkerchief inside of your spouse's pillowcase and watch God move. Do the same for your rebellious child. We have to quit putting God in a box. It is up to Him whether or not He heals, delivers, and restores the person or situation. We are the governing Body of Christ and need to be obedient to pray and do that which we know to do in faith. The rest is up to God.

There are numerous verses in the Bible that talk about anointing oil. Mark 6:13 states, "They drove out many demons and anointed many sick people with oil and healed them." In the Old Testament, God ordained anointing oil to bless His people. I recently read an article by Pastor Joseph Prince that describes how the anointing oil speaks of Christ and His finished work:

> Olive oil comes from the olive fruit. But when you press the fruit real hard, you won't find oil, only a white sap. Also, the fruit tastes very bitter. To get the oil, the fruit and its seed have to be crushed by a great weight in an olive press. The crushing also removes the bitterness. In the same manner, Jesus was crushed under the burden and weight of our sins and under the judgment of a holy

God. He was crushed to become the anointing oil that heals us today.

God is bringing the church to a place where we see the importance of the holy anointing oil. God's way is always for us to act on what we can do in the natural, and He will accomplish in the supernatural what we cannot. Using the anointing oil is biblical and ordained by God. So don't let people tell you that you are superstitious for using the anointing oil.[1]

James 5:14–15 boldly proclaims, "Is anyone among you sick? Let them call the elders of the church to pray over them and anoint them with oil in the name of the Lord. And the prayer offered in faith will make the sick person well; the Lord will raise them up. If they have sinned, they will be forgiven." This is a biblical concept. It isn't the oil that does the healing. James states that it is the prayer of faith that will save the sick, and *the Lord* will raise them up. As the Ekklesia, we must take every tool the Lord is giving us and begin implementing it all for His glory in people's lives. God is releasing strategy and keys to the Kingdom in this new season. Let's embrace all that He has for us with an open heart.

## *Activation*

A couple of years ago my husband stated that he was going to go out and walk the property lines. I had never heard him say that before and asked him what he meant. He said he was going to walk around the perimeter of our property, checking all fencing and posts to make sure no repairs were needed. I stopped him on his way out the door, handed him a bottle of anointing oil, and asked him to pray and anoint the fence posts as he walked. I anointed his shoes with oil and decreed over him Joshua 1:3: "I have given you every place where the sole of your foot will tread" (BSB) and 1 Kings 5:4: "But now the LORD my God has given me peace on every side; I have no enemies, and all is well" (NLT). Both of these verses have come to pass in our lives.

A recent testimony I would like to share is of a friend who was experiencing numerous nightmares, as were her children. I encouraged her to go through her house and anoint her windows and doorposts with oil, while welcoming angelic presence and commanding all demonic presence to go in the name of Jesus. She took the little bottle of oil and walked through her home praying in each room. She made a cross over each window and door of her home with the oil. The nightmares subsided soon after that. This story reminded me of the Passover in the Old Testament when the Lord told the Israelites to take the blood of a lamb and place it over the sides and tops of the doorframes on their houses. The Israelites were in bondage and the Lord was going to deliver them from the hand of their enemy. He said,

> On that same night I will pass through Egypt and strike down every firstborn of both people and animals, and I will bring judgment on all the gods of Egypt. I am the LORD. The blood will be a sign for you on the houses where you are, and when I see the blood, I will pass over you. No destructive plague will touch you when I strike Egypt. (Exodus 12:12–13)

Throughout history we see God using miraculous intervention to save His people. Anointing your home, your family members, and your property lines is a powerful biblical strategy to implement when the enemy attempts to attack your household.

For those of you wondering where to find anointing oil, you can purchase it online or make your own. See the endnotes for a recipe.[2]

Pray with me:

Lord, thank You for Your wisdom. Thank You for revelation. Thank You for keys that unlock spiritual truths. Thank You for sharing Your heart, Your love, Your peace, and Your joy with us. Thank You that You don't leave us to wallow in our humanness, but that You reach out of heaven with Your precious gifts and strategies. Thank You for blessing us with hope. Thank You for the tools You give us to bring healing, deliverance, and restoration to a lost generation. Thank You for choosing to use us, in our brokenness, to be vessels of love to those who need You. May we never take for granted the high calling You have placed in each one of us. May we, Your Ekklesia, be faithful to the call. We love You and praise Your name. Amen.

CHAPTER 11

# Fast for Breakthrough

*"Even now," declares the LORD, "return to Me with all your heart, with fasting and weeping and mourning."*

Joel 2:12

The father was helpless. He was desperate. He did not know what to do. His young son suffered from epilepsy. He was beside himself as he had to watch his little boy suffer day after day with horrible seizures. The seizures were so forceful and severe that the boy would often be thrown into the fire where the family cooked their food. Other times he would be thrown into the river. Can you imagine the desperation? This boy must have been covered with burn marks. He must have been traumatized from the near-drowning experiences. The father came begging at Jesus' feet, "Lord, please show Your tender mercy toward my son." (Matthew 17:15, TPT). Jesus told the father to bring the boy to Him. "Jesus rebuked the demon and it came out of him and the boy was instantly healed!" (Matthew 17:18, TPT).

Later in this passage we see the disciples asking Jesus in private why they had not been able to help the boy. They had performed many other miracles and were confidently operating in the authority given to them by Jesus. We read Jesus' response in Matthew 17:20–21:

> It was because of your lack of faith. I promise you, if you have faith inside of you no bigger than the size of a small mustard seed, you can say to this mountain, "Move away from here and go over there," and you will see it move! There is nothing you couldn't do! But this kind of demon is cast out only through prayer and fasting. (TPT)

Wow! Do you long for the faith to move mountains? I know I do. I say that I do, but am I willing to sacrifice? As the Ekklesia, we should be operating in this kind of faith each and every day. Yet this is by far the most difficult chapter I will write in this book. I have started it and deleted it numerous times. The Lord keeps convicting me as to what a powerful tool fasting is. I keep trying to convince Him that it doesn't really need to be in this book. As you probably know by now, God always wins. Consequently, here is my humble attempt to write this chapter extending God's heart for the spiritual implications behind fasting as a heavenly strategy.

For me, fasting is probably one of the hardest things I have tried to implement in my spiritual journey. Each time I fail I have cried out to God, "I can't do it!" You see, I need food. And the minute I try to go without it, I become irritable, tired, cranky, queasy, shaky, grouchy, and downright unpleasant to be around. I have heard of people who have done 40-day water only fasts, and I think they must be superhuman. I can barely fast one meal without complaining. I understand that some people cannot fast due to health conditions, and I totally respect that. That was always my excuse. But now that the Lord has been healing me up, that no longer works for me. For those who have health conditions in which fasting would truly harm you, I challenge you to look at fasting something other than food, something that you are extremely fond of. I have friends who take an extended leave from social media to draw closer to God. Others may choose to give up something they are addicted to—like sugar, caffeine, or television—for an extended period of time. God will honor everything we choose to give up in a fast consecrated to Him.

Why fast? There are many biblical examples of fasting in order to hear from God or receive breakthrough. One of my favorites was touched on in the third chapter of this book when writing about Jehoshaphat. In 2 Chronicles 20:2–4, we see that King Jehoshaphat was surrounded by enemies on all sides. The account reads:

> People came and told Jehoshaphat, "A vast number from beyond the Dead Sea and from Edom has come to fight against you; they are already in Hazazon-tamar" (that is, En-gedi). Jehoshaphat was afraid, and he resolved to seek the LORD. Then *he proclaimed a fast for all Judah,* who gathered to seek the LORD. They even came from all the cities of Judah to seek Him. (HSCB; emphasis mine)

Just picture it. Can you imagine several nations coming against the United States of America? As we see them coming, our president calls for a fast, and the whole nation fasts and seeks the Lord. Wouldn't that be an awesome sight? As we read in this biblical account, you can't go wrong when your whole nation comes before God and sacrifices. God intervened, caused confusion, and turned the enemies of Judah against each other! Such powerful intervention, released through fasting, prayer, and worship.

Another favorite biblical account is that of Queen Esther. If you have never read or studied the book of Esther, give yourself a treat this week. This story is the fabulous narration of how a Jewish orphan girl, raised by her cousin, finds miraculous favor from the Lord, becomes queen, and ultimately saves her nation from a thick plot to abolish the Jewish race from the face of the earth.

We find the account of the supernatural weapon Esther used in verse 4:16. Here, Esther says to her cousin, "Go and assemble all of the Jews who can be found in Susa and fast for me. Don't eat or drink for three days, day or night… I will go to the king even if it is against the law. If I perish, I perish" (HCSB). On the third day, we learn that as Esther stood before the king, he extended his golden scepter toward her, sparing her life. She approached and touched the tip of the scepter. "'What is it, Queen Esther?' the king asked her. 'Whatever you want, even to half the kingdom, will be given to you'" (Esther 5:3, HCSB).

This is an incredible story of bravery, sacrifice, and mercy. Esther knew what she was up against. She knew that if she went and stood before the king without an invitation, she would be killed unless he extended his scepter toward her. She risked everything with her selfless sacrifice to save her people from extinction. Esther knew that she could not do this in her own power, so she called for all of the people in her region to fast. God honored their sacrifice and intervened.

## The Grace to Fast

Are you up against something so big that you can't imagine a solution? Are you ready to throw in the towel on your marriage? Have you been diagnosed with a chronic or terminal

> *Your fast is a holy, pleasing fragrance sent up to the Lord.*

illness? Are you pressing in for the return of your prodigal child? Have you been overcome by a secret addiction that has taken you captive? Are you on the frontlines of reform for your region, state, or nation? Are you facing resistance in your church or ministry? Don't give up! The Lord has the answer to every problem you are encountering, but sometimes He requires a sacrifice. Ask Him for the grace to fast. We need to get ourselves whole and healthy so we can function as the true Ekklesia. We need to arise to begin taking back territory from the enemy for our families, cities, states, and nations.

Choose something to offer up to God and watch as you receive breakthrough. Your fast is a holy, pleasing fragrance sent up to the Lord. He looks at what you give up for Him as a beautiful aroma. He honors your offering of love.

Let me be clear. We don't fast to get something. We fast to draw near to God and to align our hearts with His. As we deprive our flesh, it causes us to press in with greater submission to the Holy Spirit. In this way we get to know Him more intimately. We become more clearly able to decipher His voice from our own voice and the voice of the enemy. Our dependence upon Him aligns us with His plans and purposes.

Many of the great healing evangelists and revivalists implemented an extended fast before their ministries actually took off and exploded. Their breakthrough occurred after their sacrifice and offering to the Lord. God loves our sacrifices, however large or small. It isn't about the act. It isn't even about whether or not you are successful in what you set out to do. Rather, it is about the heart. God knows your heart. Give it to Him and draw closer in intimacy as you spend time fasting.

You may have heard about the infamous Daniel Fast, but some of you may not know exactly where this term comes from. In the Bible, we read about a brave young man named Daniel who fasted on at least two different occasions with dramatic results. In Daniel 1, we see that Daniel and his three faithful friends were selected to train to serve in the king's palace. Daniel and his friends chose to turn down the king's choice food, and instead eat only vegetables, and drink only water for ten days. At the end of the ten days we discover that,

> God gave these four young men knowledge and understanding in every kind of literature and wisdom. Daniel also understood visions and dreams of every kind. At the end of the time that the king had said to present them, the chief official presented them to Nebuchadnezzar. The king interviewed them, and among all of them, no one was found equal to Daniel, Hananiah, Mishael, and Azariah. So they began to serve in the king's court. In every matter of wisdom and understanding that the king consulted them about, he found them 10 times better than all the diviner-priests and mediums in his entire kingdom. (Daniel 1:17–20, HCSB)

Daniel and his friends chose not to defile themselves with the king's food or with the wine he drank, and the Lord honored their decision and sacrifice. Their fast from choice food for the ten days of training made them stand far above any others in the kingdom. In fact, they were found *ten times better* in every matter of wisdom and understanding!

In Daniel 10, we read another account of Daniel fasting for three weeks. On the twenty-first day, an angel of the Lord appeared to Daniel: "'Don't be afraid, Daniel,' he said to me, 'for from the first day that you purposed to understand and to humble yourself before your God, your prayers were heard. I have come because of your prayers'" (Daniel 10:12, HCSB). I find it interesting that God heard Daniel's prayers from the moment he began to pray, but it was the fast that finally broke through the spiritual battle he was facing. We can hear God more clearly when we fast and pray. Miracles happen. God moves. Ask God to move mountains, tear down strongholds, usher in His healing and salvation, and restore His perfect will as you implement a fast and pray.

In Isaiah 58:6–9 (TPT), the Lord spells out the kind of fast that pleases Him:

> This is the kind of fast that I desire:
> Remove the heavy chains of oppression!
> Stop exploiting *your workers*!
> Set free the crushed and mistreated!
> Break off every yoke of bondage!
> Share your food with the hungry!
> Provide for the homeless
> and bring them into your home!
> Clothe the naked!
> Don't turn your back on your own flesh and blood!
> Then my favor will bathe you in sunlight
> until you are like the dawn bursting through a dark night.
> And then suddenly your healing will manifest.
> You will see your righteousness march out before you,
> and the glory of Yahweh will protect you from all harm!
> Then Yahweh will answer you when you pray.
> When you cry out for help, he will say,
> "I am here."

Pray with me:

Lord, we are Your bride. We want to experience deep intimacy with You. Make us a holy people, chosen and consecrated for Your purposes. Give us the grace to fast. Break through for us! Raise us up to be overflowing vessels of Your grace and mercy to the nations. Shift our perspectives from inward thinking to the outward mind of Christ. Let us see with Your eyes and hear with Your ears as we partner with You to bring heaven to earth. May Your Ekklesia arise in victory! Set us apart just as You set apart Daniel and his friends and made them ten times better than everyone around them. In the mighty name of Jesus we pray. Amen.

CHAPTER 12

# Become a Radically Generous Giver

*And my God will meet all your needs according to the riches of His glory in Christ Jesus.*

Philippians 4:19

It was a Tuesday morning and I sat down at my desk to pay the bills. As I picked up the pen to write out the usual $50 check to support an orphan girl in Africa, I heard the still small voice of the Lord telling me to give more. I began arguing with God in my head: *Lord, You know that I have two kids in college and their next tuition payment of $4,200.00 is due on Friday.* (As if God didn't know that!) *How much exactly were You thinking?* I about passed out as I clearly heard *$1,500* *dollars.* The argument continued: *Okay, God, but is that on top of the $50 dollars, or can I subtract that?* As I heard that last thought, I recognized how ridiculous my question must have sounded and thanked Him for always being so patient with me. I made the check out for $1,550.00, placed it in an envelope, sealed and addressed the envelope, and said a prayer. I was nervous about telling my husband what I had done. I was not working at the time and finances were tight, yet I knew in my heart that I had to be obedient to God.

The next few days were a bit rough emotionally since I wasn't used to keeping things from my husband but hadn't yet found the right moment to break the news to him. Friday rolled around and I still hadn't told him about the money I had given away. He came home from work and handed me his paycheck with a funny grin on his face. I opened it up and saw that he had received an unexpected $6,000.00 bonus. I was astounded! As we sat down for dinner, I recounted to him what had occurred on Tuesday, confessed, and apologized for not telling him sooner. We rejoiced at God's faithfulness. He not only gave us the college tuition amount that was due, but He gave us extra money to give back to Him for His Kingdom purposes. God had just demonstrated His overwhelming love and faithfulness. I was learning another biblical strategy—that a person cannot out-give God.

Malachi 3:10 boasts, "'Bring the whole tithe into the storehouse, that there may be food in My house. Test Me in this,' says the LORD Almighty, 'and see if I will not throw open the floodgates of heaven and pour out so much blessing that there will not be room enough to store it.'" My husband and I had always been regular tithers and givers, but this miracle shifted something in my perspective. That day I determined that I wanted to become radically generous. I asked the Lord to turn me into not just a radical giver but one who gives with pure joy.

Two months later I received an email from the founder of the orphanage that we had been supporting in Africa. He was

> As children of God, we have all access to His heavenly resources.

thanking us for the timely financial gift. His father had passed away. Being the extremely influential leader that he is, the whole region had come out for his father's memorial service. He told us that the donation had covered the entire cost of the funeral and fed every guest! That, my friends, is the power of being in tune with the voice of the Lord and responding with our humble *yes*. God was orchestrating a miracle behind the scenes to make provision for His servant in Africa while teaching His daughter in the United States of America a massive lesson in obedience, one that shot my faith through the roof.

## *Kingdom Thinking*

As children of God, we have all access to His heavenly resources. Matthew 6:33 says, "But seek first the Kingdom of God and His righteousness, and all these things will be given to you as well." Does this Scripture say that *some* things will be given to us? No! It says *all* things. "All things" signifies *everything* we need. As the Ekklesia and heirs to the throne, God will provide for and meet our every need. We will never be in want or lack. That is what His Word says, so why are so many believers experiencing devastating financial struggles?

Whenever somebody asks me to pray for a financial deficit, one of the first questions I ask them is whether or not they tithe. Usually the answer goes something like this: "Well, not regularly" or "I give when I can" or "I want to, but there isn't anything left after paying the bills." It is important that we understand Kingdom living when discussing tithing and giving. Kingdom thinking is upside-down compared to how most of the world lives:

- The world says to stress out. Jesus says, "Peace I leave with you" (John 14:27).

- The world says to pay your bills and then use the rest of your money on whatever you desire (that is, if there is any money left over). God says, "'Bring the whole tithe into the storehouse, that there may be food in My house. Test Me in this,' says the LORD Almighty, 'and see if I will not throw open the floodgates of heaven and pour out so much blessing that there will not be room enough to store it'" (Malachi 3:10).

- The world says to scream, shout, cuss, and get revenge. God says, "Be kind to one another, tenderhearted, forgiving one another, as God in Christ forgave you" (Ephesians 4:32, ESV).

- The world says to cry, pout, have anxiety, and be depressed when we face a crisis. God says to rejoice in the Lord always (Philippians 4:4) and "Give thanks in all circumstances..." (1 Thessalonians 5:18).

- The world says, "I'm an alcoholic," "I'm gay and was born this way," "My father died young, I guess I will too." God's Word says, "For we know that our old self was crucified with Him so that the body ruled by sin might be done away with, that we should no longer be slaves to sin" (Romans 6:6). "But you are a chosen people, a royal priesthood, a holy nation, God's special possession, that you may declare the praises of Him who called you out of darkness into His wonderful light" (1 Peter 2:9).

- The world says, "I have no choice," "I am at their mercy," "Whatever happens, happens." The Bible says, "The steps of *a good man* are ordered by the LORD" (Psalm 37:23, KJV).

Looking at this list, God's way seems to have a much better outcome. It may go against our fleshly nature, but the more time we spend with Him, and the more we begin to implement His strategies, the more we begin to see with spiritual eyes. Peace floods our souls in even the most chaotic of situations. We begin to live the supernatural life that we read about in the Bible.

Now let's look at the financial application of this upside-down thinking. Have you ever known those people with the biggest, most generous hearts? They seem to never be without. They give and they give and they keep getting more. Well, this is because they understand and implement the biblical strategy of Kingdom finances. They have become the funnel for God to flow through. You truly cannot out-give God. This is a strategy you can begin implementing immediately even when you think there is nothing to give. You will experience the miraculous in your own life as you begin breaking off the chains of poverty and lack that have bound you through the generations. Once we realize and acknowledge that everything we have belongs to the Lord, it makes it very easy to release it and give it back with a joyful heart.

## God is Faithful

Last year, my husband and I sat on the couch reminiscing, as our youngest was about to graduate from college. We rejoiced with thankful hearts as we sent off our last college tuition payment. It was a bittersweet moment in time as we pondered the faithfulness of the Lord. Ten years ago, we sent our oldest child off to a private university. Three years later, our second child went off to a private university. Three years after that, our youngest child also decided to attend a private university. Looking back over the years we stand in awe of our God who has been our most faithful provider. Logically speaking, if we were to write out our budget from the past ten years on paper, it would not add up. Most of those years, I was only able to work part time, if at all, due to chronic illness. Yet we never missed a payment and came out the other side debt-free. Only God could pull off a miracle like that! Private school tuition in the United States of America for three children on mostly one income over ten years, plus thousands of dollars in medical bills going out each year. Only God!

I do not write to boast. This has nothing to do with my husband and me. This has everything to do with God's Word and His truth. As we are faithful to give to God first, He has always been faithful to meet our every need. If we had waited to give to God after paying all of the bills, there would never have been anything left. It is a total trust thing. Do I believe the Word of God? Do I step out in faith to give of my first fruits? Yes! And when I do, there is always enough, never a lack. It boils down to this question. Can I afford to give? The answer: I can't afford not to!

## It all Gets Left Behind

The past four months have been extremely difficult as my dear mother passed away very unexpectedly. She was vibrant, healthy, fun, and super active. Her death was shocking, to say the least. Circumstances in my life escalated quite rapidly due to her sudden passing. My world seemed to be spinning out of control. While grieving and trying to stay afloat emotionally, my mind would reminisce through the years as I sorted through Mom's belongings. One thought played over and over in my mind: It doesn't boil down to what you have acquired. You can't take any of it with you. My family and I were thrust into having to decide what to do with all of Mom's earthly possessions.

The Lord brought to mind how often we strive for things—the next new toy, appliance, piece of furniture, vehicle, television, house, cell phone, computer, etc. In the end, it all gets left behind. I thought about the years I had spent striving, pursuing "things" rather than the heart of God. Through my mother's passing, my Father in heaven was gently reminding me that the only thing we can take with us when we die is other people. All the years we strive for that next promotion, that next desire, or that next treasure; none of it matters in the end. The only thing that truly matters is who I shared the love of Jesus with. John 3:3 says, "Very truly I tell you, no one can see the Kingdom of God unless they are born again."

How many people did I pass by and not stop to share the love of Jesus with? How many years did I spend being about my own business, rather than being about His business? I remember sitting at the bedside of a dying friend a few years ago. In that tender moment, as she was passing from earth to eternity, she spoke out, "None of it matters. It just doesn't matter." I believe that as she was seeing the face of Jesus, she was trying to give us a message. All of the things we consume ourselves with, all of the things we worry and stress over—in the end, none of it matters. When we meet our Savior face to face, none of it will matter: "The world and its desires pass away, but whoever does the will of God lives forever" (1 John 2:17).

I ponder in my heart the story of the precious widow in the Bible who gave everything she had out of her poverty. This beautiful woman understood Kingdom finances and ultimately knew who her provider was. She may have been poor in the world's eyes, but she was rich in the Kingdom of God.

> Jesus sat down opposite the place where the offerings were put and watched the crowd putting their money into the temple treasury. Many rich people threw in large amounts. But a poor widow came and put in two very small copper coins, worth only a few cents. Calling His disciples to Him, Jesus said, "Truly I tell you, this poor widow has put more into the treasury than all the others. They all gave out of their wealth; but she, out of her poverty, put in everything—all she had to live on."
> (Mark 12:41–44)

What does this story teach us? That God sees the heart. Many people were giving money that day. The Scripture says that the rich were throwing in large amounts. The widow's money added up to nothing in the world's eyes, and yet Jesus said she gave more than all the others. She understood Kingdom finances and knew she could not out-give God. She believed that if she gave all she had, her needs would be met. God looks at the heart, and this story reveals that He adores a heart of sacrifice.

Let's pray:

Lord, help us to become radical givers. Allow us to view our finances through Your eyes. We are only stewards of the gifts You give to us. Everything we have belongs to You. Let us become conduits of Your blessings to everyone around us. Let us see a need and give without hesitation. Forgive us for being all about ourselves. Help us to understand that as we give, we are actually storing up treasures for ourselves in heaven. Matthew 6:19–21 says, "Do not store up for yourselves treasures on earth, where moths and vermin destroy, and where thieves break in and steal. But store up for yourselves treasures in heaven, where moths and vermin do not destroy, and where thieves do not break in and steal. For where your treasure is, there your heart will be also." Help us to understand that life on this earth is extremely short. Give us hearts that desire to store up treasure in heaven where we will spend eternity with You. Change our mindset. Allow us to see the bigger picture. Let Your Ekklesia arise to become conduits of Your Kingdom economy to bless and shift the destiny of nations for Your glory. In Jesus' name we pray. Amen.

CONCLUSION

# Your Call to Action

Do you feel a stirring in your heart? Do you know you were created to live life with passion and purpose? It's time to rise up to become part of something much greater than yourself! When the Lord called you, saved you, set you free, redeemed you, restored you, healed you, and marked you for Himself, everything changed. You became part of a movement. You were chosen to fulfill something that only you can fulfill. Yet you are also part of a much bigger picture. You are a critical piece of God's redemptive plan. You are the Ekklesia, and it is time to arise to your destiny!

Many of you have become weary. You have encountered a severe attack from the enemy. You keep getting slammed. That is because you are a huge threat to his agenda! I decree Galatians 6:9 over you: "Do not become weary in doing good, for at the proper time you will reap a harvest if you do not give up" (paraphrased).

The strategies in this book are not rules or regulations. They are gifts from God, guidelines to help you walk out the immense calling on your life. God gave us a road map. He gave us principles to live by. These are in no way to hinder us, but rather to set us free. Psalm 91:1–2 promises, "Whoever dwells in the shelter of the Most High will rest in the shadow of the Almighty. I will say of the LORD, 'He is my refuge and my fortress, my God, in whom I trust.'" Begin dwelling and resting in Him. He will do wonders in and through you.

What are the desires the Lord has put on your heart? What are you wired to fulfill? You have an individual calling, but you also have a corporate calling on your life. The corporate call is that of partnering with the Ekklesia. You are an integral part of God's government here on earth. So many of our freedoms have been stripped away because we have laid down our call. We have become so consumed with the entanglements of life that we have far swayed from our first love.

**The Lord is wooing us back to His heart. We are His bride. We are His church. We are the Ekklesia! It's time to arise, unite, engage His strategies, and be transformed from survivor status to victors who move mountains, pull down strongholds, shift atmospheres, and change destinies. That is who we are marked to be.**

God is raising up His chosen ones who will not be contaminated by the world system or the shifting culture. The children of God will walk in the very nature of Christ. We will manifest His heart and the fruits of His Spirit everywhere we go.

There is currently a battle in the Body of Christ between the flesh and the Spirit. God is looking for His faithful ones, those who are willing to die to the flesh and be filled to overflowing with His Spirit.

# Your Call to Action

> For the eyes of the LORD run to and fro throughout the whole earth, to show Himself strong on behalf of *those* whose heart *is* loyal to Him.
> (2 Chronicles 16:9 NKJV)

God is looking for His yielded lovers, those surrendered to His Word and His ways, children who allow His Spirit to flow freely from their innermost being. May we become a holy stream of life, pure and set apart for the greater purpose. May intimacy with our creator become dearer to us than any other relationship, success, dream, or vision.

May we become a people who lose our own voice so that when we open our mouths, we roar with His voice! May His voice in us become so loud that it is heard across the land. May He give us every place where the soles of our feet tread (Deuteronomy 11:24).

> "May God arise, may His enemies be scattered…"
> Psalm 68:1

Your call to action is to engage with a people who are part of the Ekklesia. These are individuals who live with purpose, believers who run with vision, brothers and sisters who engage in strategy, ones who move forward in victory, implementing the Kingdom of God in their circle of influence—regional, national, or worldwide. You are a unique piece of the puzzle and you are vital to the Body of Christ. Activate your giftings and move forward in victory! It's time to arise!!!

I decree Isaiah 30:21 over you:

**Whether you turn to the right or to the left, your ears will hear a voice behind you, saying, "This is the way; walk in it."**

# Discussion Points

Chapter 1

**Prophesy**

1. Have you ever had an urge rise up within you to go up to a stranger and give them a word of encouragement, exhortation, or comfort?

2. Did you act upon that urging or did you ignore it and walk away? How did you feel when you made that choice?

3. Have you ever prophesied over somebody? Share one example of what it looked and felt like.

4. What's the worst thing that could happen if you give a word and the person rejects it? Would you still consider it worth the risk?

5. What's the best thing that could happen if you give a word and the person embraces it?

6. Practice prophesying over one another. Keep it simple! Don't overthink it! Start with a time of silence, asking God to give you something from His heart to speak to another. Then open your mouth to encourage, exhort, or comfort.

Discussion Points

## Chapter 2

**Decree the Word**

1. In what ways do you identify with Merri's story?
2. Have you spoken something negative and seen it come to pass?
3. Share your thoughts regarding decreeing the Word of God.
4. Name a time when you spoke something positive over your future and it came to pass.
5. In what way does Stuart's testimony bear witness with your spirit?
6. Choose a Bible verse to begin decreeing over your life, family, state, or nation. Write it on a notecard and carry it with you. Begin memorizing the Scripture, inserting your name, a family member's name, your state, or your nation where appropriate. Share the Scripture with your group and tell them why you chose this particular verse.

## Chapter 3

### Worship

1. What is your favorite type of worship music (hymns, contemporary Christian, gospel, rap, etc.)?

2. Do you have a favorite song that immediately lifts your spirit when you hear it? Share it with the group.

3. Download a few songs onto your phone to have at your immediate disposal when you are struggling to combat darkness. Share these songs with your group. (A few of my favorite groups are Jesus Culture, Bethel Worship, Bryan and Katie Torwalt, and Elevation Worship.)

4. Begin to read and meditate on the book of Psalms. David pours out his heart to God in song. Sing through the Psalms putting your own melody to the words. Share your favorite Psalm with the group.

5. Read 2 Chronicles 20:1–30. Discuss as a group.

6. Sing a song of worship together. Enter into His courts with praise!

# Discussion Points

## Chapter 4

### Pray

1. Share a time in which God clearly answered one of your prayers.

2. Do you believe that God always answers prayer? Discuss.

3. Have you ever said or believed the phrase, "All we can do is pray"? Has your view of that changed after reading this chapter? In what ways?

4. Do you have something which you have been praying a very long time for and feel that God is remaining silent? How does this chapter give you hope to keep contending?

5. Describe a story in the Bible where it seemed God did not answer somebody's prayer, only to find out later that He did.

6. Name a time in your life where God answered your prayer with a totally different solution than you had expected or desired, but the outcome was even better than you had hoped for.

7. Spend some time praying as a group for your community, state, or nation.

## Chapter 5

### Pray in the Spirit

1. Discuss your experience (positive or negative) with praying in tongues.

2. Discuss the difference between being filled with the Holy Spirit with the evidence of tongues found in Acts 2:4, versus the spiritual gift of tongues in 1 Corinthians 12:8–11.

3. When does speaking in tongues need to be followed by interpretation?

4. What are some benefits of praying in tongues?

5. Why do you feel there is confusion and fear among some believers regarding praying in tongues/praying in the Spirit?

6. Pray together for everyone in your group to receive their personal prayer language. This will seriously change your life! Don't skip this session! Do not be embarrassed to go after this gift! This will empower you to pray God's heart when you know not what to do. This will lift you out of the pit when you feel stuck, trapped, numb, or lost. God will intercede to pray things right! Begin praying the perfect will of God!

# Discussion Points

## Chapter 6

### Give Thanks

1. Name a hardship you are currently thankful for. Tell why you are thankful in the midst of this trial.

2. Testify about a time where you endured suffering, but when it was all said and done, you recognized the hand of God in it and became thankful.

3. Share a Bible story that comes to mind where the character was thankful despite his/her circumstances.

4. Some people struggle to have a thankful heart. What are some hindrances to having a heart of gratitude?

5. Is there anything you need to repent of where you found yourself whining and complaining instead of offering thanksgiving to God? Share how you could have handled the situation better.

6. Spend some time with your group thanking God for the difficult situations you currently find yourselves in. Read James 1:2–4 together and thank God that He is making you mature and complete, lacking nothing.

## Chapter 7

### Forgive

1. Share an instance in which you were wounded by betrayal.

2. Have you been able to forgive, release, and bless your betrayer(s)? If not, what is holding you back?

3. Are you willing to allow the group to pray for you to release this hold the enemy has on you? As a group, pray for anyone holding onto unforgiveness or needing deliverance from the pain of betrayal. You don't need to share details. God knows. Just pray for deliverance and the ability to forgive, release, and bless your betrayer(s).

4. Name a character in the Bible who was betrayed. How did they handle the betrayal?

5. How do you typically handle offenses?

6. Ask the Lord to reveal any offenses of the heart you may be holding on to. As a group, pray for the Lord to free each of you from offense. Pray together that you would become a people who are not affected or derailed by offense. Take up the shield of faith and determine that all future offenses will bounce off of you by the power of Jesus.

## Discussion Points

### Chapter 8

**The Blood of Jesus**

1. Did Sheri's story build your faith or stretch you in any way?

2. What is your understanding of taking communion?

3. Find one Old Testament verse that emphasizes sacrificing a pure, spotless animal to atone for your sins. Find one New Testament verse that discusses how Jesus became the ultimate atonement for your sins. Discuss with the group.

4. Choose a current situation you can immediately begin pleading the blood of Jesus over.

5. Take communion together, thanking Jesus for what He did on the cross.

6. If you are ill, begin taking communion daily as you would take medication regularly. Decree Isaiah 53:5 over yourself. Watch the blood of Jesus restore your health.

## Chapter 9

## Generational Sin and Curses

1. Ask the Lord to reveal any generational curses being carried down in your family bloodline. Write them here and share with the group.

2. Ask the Lord to forgive you and your ancestors for all known and unknown generational sins. Write out a prayer of repentance.

3. Ask the Lord to break off all generational curses and to let them end with you.

4. Plead the blood of Jesus over yourself, your children, and your grandchildren. Ask God to bless your family to the thousandth generation per His Word.

5. Search out a couple of Scriptures that speak to you regarding the areas that apply to your circumstances, e.g., health, provision, blessings and favor, protection, wisdom, etc. Write out some decrees, based on these Scriptures, to begin speaking over your family bloodline.

6. Keep track of your words during the day by carrying around a 3" x 5" card. Write the word "Positive" on one side of the card and "Negative" on the other side. Make a tally mark on the appropriate side of the card each time you catch yourself saying a positive or negative statement. When you catch yourself saying a negative remark, ask the Lord to forgive you and break off the word-curse, then move on with your day. Don't dwell on it. This will get easier and easier, and you will be amazed at the transformation of your mind. Do this a few different times throughout the next several months and watch the miracle God performs in you.

Discussion Points

Chapter 10

**Anointing Oil and Prayer Cloths**

1. What is your experience, if any, with anointing oil?

2. What is your experience, if any, with prayer cloths?

3. Share with the group one way you could immediately implement this strategy.

4. Does your church/ministry incorporate the use of anointing oil or prayer cloths? If so, do you have any testimonies to share with the group?

5. Go through your home this week and anoint your windows and doorposts with oil. Walk your property lines, anointing your fence posts with oil, and decree that only angelic presence is welcome on your property and in your home. Command all demonic influence to go in Jesus' name.

6. Have the leader of your group anoint each of you with oil and pray over you or decree a Scripture over you.

7. Have everyone bring a handkerchief or piece of fabric to your next group meeting. Anoint them with oil, place them in the center of the group, and pray over them. Encourage each person to place one in someone's pillowcase or coat pocket as you contend for them. You can also ask the Lord who to mail one to, and be obedient. Rejoice together when the testimonies come in giving glory to God!

## Chapter 11

### Fast for Breakthrough

1. What are your views on fasting?
2. Have you ever fasted for something? What was the outcome?
3. Share one failure or one victory with attempting to fast.
4. Read Daniel 1 together. Discuss.
5. What is one thing you would like to fast for in order to see breakthrough?
6. Pray for one another to have the grace to fast.

Discussion Points

## Chapter 12
### Become a Radically Generous Giver

1. What are your views on tithing?

2. Do you have any fears or inhibitions in regards to tithing? Share with the group.

3. Do you believe there is a difference between tithing in the Old Testament, and New Testament views on giving? Discuss.

4. Do you have a testimony to share with the group regarding tithing?

5. Are you willing to begin giving/tithing if you are not already doing so? If you are already tithing, are you willing to become a radically generous giver?

6. Read Galatians 6:7 together. Discuss the concept of reaping and sowing.

# Notes

**Chapter 3: Worship**
1. Jesus Culture, "Defender (Live)," YouTube video, September 4, 2018, https://www.youtube.com/watch?v=DtPgAFpkJLE
2. Michael W. Smith, "Surrounded (Fight My Battles)," YouTube video, December 28, 2017, https://www.youtube.com/watch?v=YBl84oZxnJ4.

**Chapter 4: Pray**
1. "Syria, Russia Say over 100 Missiles Fired, Many Intercepted." *The Times of Israel*, 14 Apr. 2018, www.timesofisrael.com/moscow-says-over-100-missiles-fired-at-syria-significant-number-intercepted/.

**Chapter 5: Pray in the Spirit**
1. *Smith Wigglesworth Devotional* (Kensington, PA: Whitaker House, 1999), 190.

**Chapter 6: Give Thanks**
1. *The Boy in the Striped Pajamas*, directed by David Heyman (Miramax, Heyday Films, BBC Films, 2008).
2. *Smith Wigglesworth Devotional* (Kensington, PA: Whitaker House, 1999), 46.

## Chapter 8: The Blood of Jesus
1. Bill Johnson, "Communion and the Finished Work of the Cross," YouTube video, June 19, 2017, https://www.youtube.com/watch?v=PbBPKxibjsY
2. Robert Lowry, *Nothing but the Blood of Jesus*, 1876, public domain.

## Chapter 9: Generational Sin and Curses
1. Graeme Walsh, *Generational Sin and Curses* (Thomas Nelson, Inc., 1984), 4. Used by permission.
2. Walsh, 16–17.
3. Suggested reading: Vito Rallo, *Breaking Generational Curses and Pulling Down Strongholds* (Creation House Press, 2000). Marilyn Hickey, *Breaking the Generational Curses: Overcoming the Legacy of Sin in Your Family* (Harrison House, 2001). Graeme Walsh, *Christianity and Freemasonry: Are they Compatible?* (Self-published, 2015).

## Chapter 10: Anointing Oil and Prayer Cloths
1. Joseph Prince, "Understanding the Significance of the Olive Tree and Anointing Oil," accessed June 28, 2019. https://www.josephprince.org/blog/articles/understanding-the-significance-of-the-olive-tree-and-anointing-oil.
2. Anointing Oil Recipe: Mix together 8 oz. almond oil, 1 eyedropper full of frankincense essential oil, 2 eyedroppers of myrrh essential oil, and 4 eyedroppers of cinnamon essential oil. This recipe will make a substantial amount that you can pour into small bottles to share with friends.

# About the Author

Debbie Bilek equips individuals, families, churches, ministries, schools, businesses, and governments to capture a heavenly perspective in living out God's plans and purposes for their lives. The Lord has healed her of fibromyalgia, chronic fatigue syndrome, Hashimoto's thyroiditis, Sjögren's syndrome, migraine headaches, and reflex sympathetic dystrophy. Her passion is to see people healed, delivered, and restored to their true identity. She speaks the Word of God over lives with power and authority, imparting truth and transformation. She calls forth the Ekklesia to arise and shine to bring heaven to earth. Debbie has been married for 32 years to her college sweetheart and the love of her life, Bill. They have three grown children who are destined to be world-changers.

**For more information and resources visit:**
**StrategiesFromHeaven.com**

www.ingramcontent.com/pod-product-compliance
Lightning Source LLC
LaVergne TN
LVHW011840060526
838200LV00054B/4114